The Best
I Could Do

The Best I Could Do

Sharon Parkinson

Published by Zaccmedia
www.zaccmedia.com
info@zaccmedia.com

Published September 2020

ISBN 978-1-911211-98-3
Available on Kindle

British Library Cataloguing-in-Publication Data
A catalogue record for this book is available from the British Library.

CONTENTS

(A homage to the major mainstream musical influence
in my life as a teenager - The Carpenters)

Acknowledgement

I originally started out to write a short piece for my children, to try to portray areas of my life that are difficult to talk about. How the emotional programming and destabilising experiences I went through as a child dramatically affected the way I consequently learnt to operate as an adult.

I wanted to say that it is okay if we are not perfect, if we mess up, and even spend years living life with the wrong attitude.

Some people can never change their ways and do things differently, often because they are not even aware of their conduct and that is why, when my short piece expanded and turned into a book, I included some illustrations of a negative and destructive personal relationship in my childhood which continued into my adult years.

I wanted to demonstrate that God can always turn things around. He can turn anyone's life around, no matter what sort of mess they have made of it or how it started out.

I also wanted to dispel the long-established misconception that, if you were brought up in a Christian family, everything will go well and you will have immunity from developing deep-seated issues that need dealing with later in life.

I wanted to contradict the belief that, if you do consequently have issues or are consumed by anxiety and crippled by depression as an adult, you have handled everything wrongly and that permanently guilty feeling you walk around with is entirely your own fault.

We are all weak-minded, vulnerable humans, whether we have a Christian faith and a close relationship with God, or not. And just because we are entrusted with the care and responsibility for someone else's life, in a parental role or in a spousal capacity, does not automatically transform any one of us into a super hero. All our failings are still rooted within and sometimes, the extra stress and pressure of added responsibility can release aspects of our character that even we ourselves do not want to admit to, let alone witness them being revealed to those around us.

As I have recalled my own youth, I have seen just how faithful God has always been towards me and later on towards my own family. I was a Christian but I didn't always pray when I should have. I didn't read my Bible as regularly as would have blessed my life, yet God never gave up on me.

When times of huge stress and trauma occurred in my younger days, they did not usually see me on my knees, praying. Those were invariably the times when my brain was paralysed and I was operating on autopilot. Most of the time I was getting through in my own strength, or so I thought, yet God was always, always there. He has constantly known me better than I know myself and, as I have revisited my younger self, I realised that even though I took my faith for granted, He still loved me.

*He has always loved me **unconditionally!***

The realisation of how I have always been seen in God's eyes and the concept of unconditional love being applied to *me*, not just other people, has been a huge revelation. It has only sunk into my brain and been absorbed by my conscious thought processes relatively recently, and I am still revelling in the concept.

Although God does not like our sinful behaviour and always prefers that we commune regularly with Him and allow Him to guide our lives, He still loves us just the same even when we want to do our own thing. We can never make God love us any more, or any less, by our actions. Consequently, it is never too late to turn to God or come back to God.

Therefore, I fully acknowledge that the reason I and my family have turned out the way we have has nothing at all to do with what we have achieved in our own right, but is completely and utterly due to God's unfailing provision, guidance, and faithfulness, despite my blundering attempts to do things my own way!

Prologue

We have probably all heard it said that God has a sense of humour.

Well, He was certainly exercising it when He decided to give me four innocent babies with the expectation that I would be the best person to raise them in a manner which would result in four balanced, socially acceptable, functioning adults.

Yes, I could cook and bake, so they weren't going to starve. I knew how to trawl around the best charity shops in the late 1970s and 1980s and I could knit and sew, so if the worst came to the worst, they would always have something to wear. I could (pre-children) string words together to construct sentences, so I could teach them to speak properly. I could do my best to provide them with the many practical necessities of life, but the possibility that these four little people could end up going into the rest of their lives reproducing all my quirks, obsessive compulsions, and hang-ups, through no fault of their own, seemed to me to be an excessively risky undertaking and I have wondered, since they have actually grown up, why on earth did God award me the privilege?

I had been an extremely unhappy child and was scared of most things and most people. My maternal role model for parenting had not been the best and I had a pretty skewed idea of the world by the time I was old enough to procreate. Who knows what would have happened if I had been left to my own devices?

Thankfully, God had always been there to oversee my children's emotional and spiritual wellbeing and as they grew up surrounded by Christian influences, they each developed their own relationship with Him.

However, in recent years I have felt that the day my children officially became adults, God looked at them, looked back at me, gave me a smile and said,

'Thank you very much for having them. I saw the struggles you went through and I know you did the best you could do. Remember when they were babies and you held a church service for each of them, to dedicate them back to me? Well, I'm here to reassure you that I will be continuing to watch over every aspect of their lives as they go on into their adult years.'

And so, He did. My kids were upgraded as God took each one of them, dusted off all the rubbish that had accumulated, polished them up, and sent them out into the world to be a positive influence on the people they came into contact with. What is more, He showed them how to overcome the generational hang-ups, so they were not perpetuated when bringing up their own children, in due course.

God knew that I wouldn't be offended by His takeover bid and, because I know they are in good hands, I would like to dedicate this book to my children and say,

'Congratulations on surviving my ministrations! I hope my best efforts weren't too flawed and if there are any complaints, don't all shout at once—organise a rota.'

I am also aiming to inflict maximum embarrassment on my offspring as I cobble together the reminiscent ramblings of childhood, both theirs and my own. I hope that, in view of the fact that they will have already put my name down for that long sought-after, geographically distanced, high-security, retirement home for the bewildered, their financial inheritance may be enhanced by the sales of this book and will help cover the cost of my care.

Every cloud...

CHAPTER 1

We've Only Just Begun

*Embarrassing recollections of me as a
very small child*

I have a very sketchy memory of my early years, probably because they were so long ago.

Still, two hazy recollections have filtered sufficiently through the worn out little grey cells, to evoke the memory of a sunny day when I was sitting on a garden wall watching my brother kicking a ball about and another occasion when I was sitting naked on the draining board, being bathed in the kitchen sink.

I am assuming—and very much hoping, for the sake of decency—that I was extremely young at the time, but the strange thing is, I remember both instances as if I was standing behind me, looking at the scenes as an observer.

That's a worry, don't you think?

I do distinctly remember the time, though, when we went on a family holiday to Filey on the east coast of Yorkshire. It was a Butlin's-type set up, which had basic, draughty chalets with bunk beds and there was a gap under the wooden front door you could limbo under.

I would have been around four years old, and I was playing in the playground on the swings. There was a group of older children there, and I was watching in fascination as these big, clever kids swung as high as they could, jumped off the swing at the highest point, then landed neatly and ran off laughing.

I decided that I, too, was clever enough to do that, so I followed suit. I jumped and landed. The problem was, my landing was not quite so neat. I landed on my bottom and for a split-second, I felt so proud of myself that I had done what the big kids had done.

My elation was very short-lived. The swing I had just launched myself off did what swings do and carried on its projected path, which now included the back of my head. There was a *crack*, a LOT of blood, that fraction of a second before the pain hit and possibly a lot of noise. The next thing I knew, I had been whisked off to the medical room by uniformed St John's Ambulance people, and more pain was being inflicted whilst they messed about with the gaping hole in my skull.

Yes, well, I'm prepared to admit now that it probably wasn't actually gaping but I remember it was distinctly painful, and I was seeing double of everything. There was a lot of swabbing with warm water and sutures were inserted because I was already crying, so they just got on with it. Then, to my further indignation, they put mustard on my rapidly swelling lump!

I found out later in life that it was probably iodine that was applied but at the time I was convinced it was mustard and it didn't half sting!

I still have the lump on the back of my head as a memento.

I don't recall having a lot of sore throats but I must have had recurrent tonsillitis because one day I was hauled out of the classroom when I was in the infant school and taken off to hospital. No warning and no explanation were given by my mother, but I shortly found myself inside the old PRI hospital and, worse still, on the inside of a hospital gown with a split up the back. Even then, the gowns weren't made to fit anyone in particular and this specific one managed to drown my scrawny, five-year-old frame at the same time as failing to cover up my modesty.

I remember being taunted by boys on what must have been the children's ward (although for years I thought I had been put on a boys' ward), shouting that they could see my bottom as I walked down the ward. Even at that tender age I was completely mortified.

I don't even remember whether I was told what I was in hospital for but when I came around from the anaesthetic, I realised I had had my tonsils removed. I knew this because my throat hurt like you wouldn't believe: it felt like sand had been poured down it and I couldn't talk. I think my post-operative care was on a women's ward because I remember all the nice ladies in nighties being kind to me. I was given lots of ice cream to soothe my very sore throat, and some rather wonderful chewing gum, which I assume had some medicinal, antiseptic properties. I seem to recall that cornflakes also featured in my convalescence, so it wasn't all bad.

That wasn't the only time my bottom was the cause of childhood humiliation. I was quite a bit older when I developed a boil on that sensitive region of my anatomy. I think boils and abscesses were more commonplace in times gone by, due to dietary insufficiencies.

Anyway, the consequence of my particular insufficiency started off very small and, over several days, grew very large and excruciatingly painful. So dramatic was it that the doctor was called. In those days, GPs actually made home visits on a regular basis, and it was considered normal practice for the reliable, knowledgeable family doctor to arrive, as requested, at the front door, complete with his tweed jacket and smoking his pipe!

Dr Hunt from our local surgery knew everything there was to

know about all the members of our family and could probably tell you if you were ill if he saw you in the street. He visited my boil regularly and watched it grow, making all the appropriate tutting noises and *hmmm*-ing at all the right intervals. It reached a point when the abscess development had gone on too long for his liking, and on one visit he announced that he would return the next day and lance it!

I'm not sure whether I slept or not, through fear and imaginings that night, but something must have sent a subliminal message somewhere to something, as I remember getting out of bed the following morning with very yucky, wet-feeling pyjama pants and dashing to the bathroom. My abscess had burst, releasing a remarkable amount of detritus and gunge, which left a considerable impression on the floor between my bed and the bathroom. I recall the remains of this crater taking some further time to heal completely and still involving the regular close inspections and the short-sighted peerings of our family doctor, who was determined my affliction would not recur.

Thankfully, that was the only occurrence of my boil, but my GP certainly knew me a lot better by the end of my treatment and, no doubt, remembered me for all the most embarrassing reasons.

It is interesting to compare the health service you used to get then with the service provided now.

Nowadays, the GP will do a home visit when you're dead. If you're not dead, you're fit to come into the surgery.

I seem to recall that most of my ailments, illnesses, and recuperations took place during the holidays because I had remarkably little time off school. I hated school, but I was never allowed to wangle any time off. I was sent to school complete with any infections I was incubating and if any bits of me hurt so bad it felt like they were dropping off, they would just have to drop off and be picked up later on my way home. I came home many a time with a nose bleed but only after the bell had rung for official home time.

I used to get myself ready in the morning, sometimes scraping the fantastically formed ice patterns off the inside of my bedroom window on winter days. I would walk the long journey to school because my mother had already left for work. If I was really late for school, which happened frequently, I used to cut through the woods just off the main road. That route was completely deserted and involved crossing a sort of bridge over the brook. It was invariably muddy and slippery and if anything had happened to me on that route, nobody would have known where I was.

I was supposed to wash up all the breakfast dishes before I went to school but frequently left them because I was always late in the mornings. I would come home by myself, always in fear of a local catholic school boy who used to taunt me from the other side of the road as I walked through a local housing estate. He never actually hurt me, but the fear was always there.

In the winter months, I always enjoyed looking at all the lights that were on inside other people's homes along my route. I used to imagine who lived in each lit up house and what their lives were like.

My house was always dark as I approached it, and cold when I went in, using the key which was lodged in the garden shed. To this day, I loathe coming home to a dark house. I will always leave a light on if I know it's going to be dark when I get back.

CHAPTER 2

Solitaire

I was a very lonely child

We used to live in one of the semi-detached houses at the older end of Whitefield Road in Penwortham but when I was nine years of age, we moved up to the newer, extended part of the road. This more recent build was three years old and a dormer bungalow. It was a while after we moved in before we got central heating installed, hence the frosty patterns on the inside of the bedroom window in the mornings.

As soon as I got home from school, it was my job to clear out the fire grate and check for any large cinders that could be used again. I would then carry the dead ashes very, very carefully (think egg & spoon race-type concentration) to the outside bin, and replace the empty ashpan under the grate. The new fire would be laid using screwed up newspapers, sticks, and proper coal. We had a coal bunker outside the back door and the coalman would deliver the fuel from his flat-backed lorry, wearing a leather waistcoat that was black with coal dust. He would heft several heavy sacks off his wagon and onto his shoulders, one at a time, with apparent ease and carry them up the drive and into the back garden. The contents would be tipped into the concrete bunker through the hatch at the top. Sometimes the pieces of coal would be so big they prevented the rest of the coal from being shovelled out of the sliding hatch at the bottom of the bunker. When this happened, my dad would remove the offending piece and smash it up with his lump hammer so it could be utilised.

Lighting that particular fire was always difficult and I had to use a sheet of opened out newspaper, supported by a shovel or poker, to put over the fireplace to persuade it to draw properly. This was a very hazardous practice, even for an adult, but to give a child that responsibility was positively dangerous. How that house didn't burn down, I will never know.

Whilst the fire was getting going, I then had to rush to wash up the breakfast things that I should have done before school. If they weren't done before my mother came home, I would be in big trouble. I once stole a drink of orange squash whilst I was washing up (I wasn't allowed orange squash) and was halfway through it when I heard my mother come in through the front door. I drank the rest so fast that my throat went into spasm from fear and I couldn't stop swallowing for ages afterwards. I still got into trouble over the washing up because my mother could see soap suds on the dishes, and they were still warm, so she knew I hadn't done them in the morning as I was supposed to. It wasn't enough that the job had been done. It hadn't been done when she had stipulated.

Maybe that explains why I always prefer to rinse the washed up dishes in clean water when I wash up now, although nowadays, I am allowed as much orange squash as I like!

My area of great responsibility did not just lie with fire lighting. Indeed no.

I was multi-talented. I was an *Ink Monitor*.

I was one of the chosen few at school who was deemed sensible enough to be entrusted with the huge glass bottle of dark blue ink which was kept in the classroom cupboard. Every Friday afternoon it was my job to take turns with the other Ink Monitors—I was not the only one, I don't want to boast excessively—and go around the classroom filling up all the ink wells. At junior school, we each sat in pairs at a wooden twin desk which had a sloping surface that divided into two writing areas that also doubled up as lids. We kept all our books, pencils, and crayons in the recessed compartment under the lids and this was also where we kept our prized ink pens.

These pens were not much more than smoothly shaped pieces of painted wood but they had a removable, brass nib at the writing end, which was coaxed into action by dipping it into the integral inkpot that was sunk into a hole, sited at the right-hand corner of each half of the desk. If you were left-handed, that was your problem. Left-handed writing was still very discouraged and it was believed that left-handed pupils could be retrained if only they would make the effort. We were still decades away from realising that it was not just a method of writing and that left-handed brains functioned in a completely different way from right-handed ones.

It was quite a skill, learning the art of controlling an ink pen, as the heavily ink-stained desks and school uniforms attested to. We were allowed one new nib per half-term and if a mid-half term request was made for a new one, there would be an inquest as to the cause of the demise of the old one. It usually involved it having come into contact with a fellow pupil's person and bending on impact. Not that I would know anything about that.

Our household, in common with most others in the 1960s, had strict rules when it came to performing domestic tasks. Jobs had to be done on set days and at specific times of the day and beds had to be made in the morning before we left the house. There were very few items that were disposable, so everything was washed and re-used, including any plastic bags that came into our possession.

Freshly washed clothes had to be pegged out on the washing line in a specific way, according to exacting guidelines.

Despite the fact that the outside line was used regularly, it was always wiped along its length with the dishcloth before use. No line marks were allowed to transfer to the washing. Socks had to always be pegged up by the toe, in matching pairs. I suppose the reasoning was that sock toes could be darned if holes were created, whereas if the elastic around the cuff was spoiled, that was harder to rectify. Whites were pegged with whites and, perish the thought that your neighbours would be able to see your 'unmentionables' whilst on the line, so it was common practice to peg out the underwear then drape the bed sheets around it all to enclose them and preserve the family's modesty from prying eyes.

Neighbours from all classes of the community were ready to criticise and judge the housewife's slovenliness if her whites were not whiter than white, or if they detected any hint of greying. To economise on clothes pegs, items of washing would always share a peg with the next item along and washing was never left out in the rain or overnight. Tongues would certainly have cause to wag if that happened!

I well recall waiting in line one September at junior school when it was our class's turn to move up into the next school year. This had been long dreaded by most of us who had heard all the stories about Mrs—let's just call her Teacher, to protect her guilt—and the things she did if you incurred her wrath. I can even remember that churning feeling you get, low down in your tummy when you're afraid of something that is imminent.

The stories all turned out to be true.

Mrs Teacher's mission in life was to make sure all her pupils learnt their spellings and their times tables. Her method was to give homework out, then test us the day after. She did this by making everyone stand on their chairs when the bell went for home time. She would then walk around and fire questions at her target child.

'5 x 7?'

'35, Mrs Teacher.'

She was never 'Miss'. She told us she was a married lady and would be addressed as such. We were junior school kids. We didn't care what she was, but we knew she had to be obeyed.

'Spell "Beautiful,"' she would bark.

'B-E-A-U-T-I-F-U-L, Mrs Teacher.' She wasn't, but she got results.

If we had answered correctly, we were allowed to get off our chairs one by one, turn them upside down and place them, seat down on top of the table. We did this to aid the caretaker who would be in later on to sprinkle the product that looked like damp sand and smelled like Jeyes Fluid, before he swept it all up, along with the dust and dirt it had attracted.

If there was a pupil who hadn't learnt the requested task, for whatever reason, then that child remained on their chair until the end, standing high above everyone else and was ritually humiliated by the teacher's scathing remarks about how stupid and bad they were. They were then given whatever punishment she saw fit to dole out. It certainly 'encouraged' me to learn my tables and spellings, but it was an achievement gained through fear.

Ask me any times table. Go on, ask me.

The one time I did have an extended period of time off school was when I developed rheumatic fever. It came on gradually when I was aged around nine, and got worse and worse until I couldn't walk. I would spend all day on the sofa in the dining kitchen and my dad would carry me up the stairs to bed at night, which I found quite a novelty at the time, but, thankfully, it was only temporary. Dr Hunt was, again, a regular visitor to the house, bringing with him his smoky, tweedy aura and mysterious bottles and pill boxes.

There was no patient information in those days. The dark brown dispensing bottles were labelled 'The Medicine' and the round cardboard pill boxes were labelled 'The Tablets'. It was a wonder any patient survived, really, as it would have been incredibly easy to take the wrong medication by mistake. My rheumatic fever lasted around three weeks and the symptoms gradually receded until I appeared to have fully recovered.

Later on in the term, after I had returned to school, we watched a solar eclipse through the classroom window at school and I burnt a hole in the back of my right eye, causing permanent damage. I also remember that classroom very well as having the best collection of Enid Blyton books on its bookshelves and I had read every one whilst I was off ill with rheumatic fever.

During that year, my grandad died of a heart attack, aged 84. He had been on his way to buy an engagement ring for his prospective third wife when he collapsed on a zebra crossing in Liverpool!

Grandad had lived with us for a short time a few months previously. How my dad got that one past my mother for approval is a mystery. Grandad was a kindly, gentle man, who imbibed Epsom Salts in a glass of water every morning, followed by scalding hot porridge, to which he added lots of salt. His fool proof remedy to discourage the effects of his advancing arthritis was to rub himself all over with Wintergreen Embrocation on a daily basis. Whilst these preventative measures clearly had a good effect on his health, he smelled to high heaven! He would have repelled any invading germ within a fifty-yard radius. I quite liked the tarry, spicy smell, but, boy, it was strong! None of us needed any of our own chests rubbing with anything that winter. We just used to inhale Grandad.

He would sit in the best armchair, legs akimbo, with his broadsheet newspaper also spread wide and rattle and shake it regularly whilst the rest of us were all trying to watch our black and white television set. It drove my mother wild!

We kids didn't appreciate the fact that he also sat in the same expansive manner in the back of the car when we all had to share the seat with him. It was a tight fit, to say the least.

He had lost his second wife, the only grandma I ever knew, a few years before. Although I only saw her a few times, I remember her as a sweet old lady, an archetypal, smiling, rosy-cheeked grandma, who used to knit dishcloths with ecru-coloured cotton yarn and big, wooden needles.

She was in a wheelchair by the time I knew her and her hands were all twisted. She was clearly riddled with arthritis but I don't know what she used to do in her early years which may or may not have contributed to her condition.

I vaguely remember visiting my grandad and grandma when they lived in Wiltshire. I must have been very small as I just have a hazy recollection of a vegetable garden, an old stone cottage with a twisty staircase and pale yellow, brushed cotton pyjamas with penguins on (mine, not his).

Grandad spent the last years of his life dividing his time between his grown up children and their families. He even went to Canada by ship to live with his daughter for a while. He had returned to England to live with my Uncle and Auntie in Widnes, where he had obviously met up with a lady, with whom he was preparing to settle down, but didn't get the chance to as things turned out.

Fear was the overriding emotion of my childhood. I had regular, repetitive nightmares and used to wake up rigid with terror but unable to scream. I still have the vision of my red night light that was attached to the main light bulb on my bedroom ceiling. I would lie there, filled with terror, staring at that red light until the fear gradually receded. I can still remember two of those dreams in detail, but they make no more sense now than they did then.

One involved a grey, stone building with a flight of stone steps descending from a door on the outside wall. There would be dozens of cats and dogs all tumbling over each other down these steps.

That was it, but something about it terrified me.

The second nightmare I recall, although I'm sure there were others, featured a tree-lined suburban avenue. An old, bent over, witch-like hag would stand on the corner of the street with a knobbly tree branch for a walking stick. She was on the opposite side of the road to where I was walking.

Again, that was it.

There is probably some deep, psychological explanation for these seemingly simple tableaux that are still in my mind but I have no idea why they were so petrifying at the time.

I was the youngest of three children. My brother was nearly six years older than me and my sister was exactly four years older. Because there were only sixteen months in age between my brother and sister, they tended to have the same circle of friends at school and church and spent a lot of their leisure time together.

As a consequence, I was left on my own most of the time and I did feel very detached from the rest of my family. I was a painfully shy child and struggled to fit in or feel like I achieved anything.

I even missed out on the one sporting event at school that I had coveted since I was aware of its existence. I hated sports with a passion. I was flat-footed and, even in my nightmares, I could not run to save my life.

However, during the last sports day of their junior school career, it was a tradition that the class who were soon to leave to go on to Secondary School were given the special privilege of partaking in the Obstacle Course. This event did not require speed or stamina but rather skill and technique, so I was definitely up for it. There were no practice runs, though, because it was all the elderly caretaker could do to lay out all the obstacles for one afternoon per year, never mind in the days running up to the occasion.

The race was about to begin and we were all lined up in our P.E. kits, ready to sprint off and start wriggling and climbing when it was our turn. I assumed the position of an efficient athlete, waiting for the signal. The whistle blew to indicate the time had come to experience my one and only moment of sporting prowess.

This was it! I set off, promptly tripped over a blade of grass, or some other non-existent hazard, fell over, and was carted off to the sidelines where I had to sit and watch everyone else have their five minutes of fame. I distinctly remember crying my eyes out and it wasn't because of my injuries.

My aversion to all things sporty extended to the weekly school trips to the swimming baths at Kirkham. I hated the prospect of these afternoons and anticipated them with dread. Not only was I expected to take all my clothes off in the tiny, fairly grubby looking cubicles and put on a swimming suit that fit where it touched, but I was expected to do it quickly and in the depths of freezing cold temperatures. Cold water held no appeal for me—not much has changed there—and deep water with lots of people who couldn't be trusted not to grab me by the legs and pull me under was yet another thing in my life that I was afraid of. I somehow bluffed my way through the swimming lessons, making half-hearted attempts at doggy paddling whilst supported by bright orange, plastic armbands, but the worst part of the trip, by far, was the humiliation of always taking the longest time to get dry and dressed. I could never drag my clothes quickly on to damp skin, so consequently, I was invariably the last one to board the school bus for the return journey and the jeers of my fellow classmates would be ringing in my ears for the rest of the afternoon.

There was an event that I remember with fondness, however, and that was when I was involved in one of the older classes who got to do a group dance for a summer open day at school. There were a lot of dressing up outfits involved, and we waved copious amounts of gauzy, nylon, see-through scarves around to the accompaniment of the James Bond films' theme music.

Generally though, I hated school and found it difficult to make friends. School friends were not encouraged at our house. Any visitors to the house were my mother's choice, so they were few and far between.

My overall memories of childhood are ones of hiding in my bedroom, curled up under the bedcovers, and reading by torchlight, even during daylight hours. Or sleeping: when you sleep, the world goes away.

My mother used to shout upstairs to ask what I was doing. My stock answer was 'Just tidying my bedroom,' but I never was. It seemed as if whatever I was doing was wrong. Living with that awareness made me feel constantly on edge. I have realised since my mother died a few years ago that I spent all my life not only fearful but permanently physically tense.

When I made that realisation, it explained so much to me about the many physical issues that I developed as time went on and the fact that I have always dealt with conflict by withdrawing and shutting myself off. That is what I did as a child, because that way, I was out of everybody's sight and less likely to incur further wrath.

I would go on long bike rides or spend hours on my roller skates going up and down the pavements or exploring in fields.

When I was growing up in Penwortham, there were fields behind our house for as far as you could see and it was only after I left and got married that the primary school was built and further housing developments changed the area beyond recognition. I remember once going into a field to talk to a horse that was there. After I turned to go home, I realised that not only was the horse following me but it had also attracted a herd of cows who were now trotting along behind.

I was so scared and ran so fast to get to the field stile and jump over to safety. I wasn't as keen on going horse visiting after that.

If only there had been an 'Escape from Advancing Cows' event in the school sports day. I would have won a medal and earned my five minutes of fame, for sure.

CHAPTER 3

Top of the World

*The dubious delights of the chemical
toilet at the top of the hill*

My mother had been born into a strict Salvation Army family. Unfortunately, her mother was not married at the time, which, in 1929, was considered a very shameful state of affairs and my mother grew up with this stigma. I don't think her mother was ostracised from her family, as was sometimes the case in those days, but it was all a bit of a taboo subject on the whole.

Apparently, my grandmother could be a violent woman and, from the little I did glean, it sounded like she suffered from bipolar with manic depression. I was told that she would throw shoes at my mother from across the room and when my mother grew up and had her own kitchen, she would never have sharp knives on a rack on the wall: they would always be put away in a drawer, out of immediate reach. I think her mother would just grab whatever was nearest to hand, so it had been in my mother's interests to keep potentially dangerous objects out of sight.

When my mother was still a child, my grandmother married a man who already had two daughters. Her mother and stepfather subsequently went on to have two little boys. The acquisition of step-sisters and half-brothers seemed to have made my mother very bitter, and she despised her stepfather, even though it sounded to me like he was a good man who formally adopted her, and she took his surname.

My grandma had been a confectioner. In her younger days, she had been employed in a bakery and apparently, she made the most marvellous cakes and pastries. Years later, she became a boarding house landlady in Blackpool and that is when my mother began attending a church in the area called Jubilee Temple. That was where she met my dad. After they got married in 1949, they lived in a two-roomed flat in Blackpool. This modest accommodation was quite common for those days when newly married folk started off with what they could afford, which was usually very little, and then they would gradually improve their living arrangements as they managed to save up.

After my mother got married, I don't think she had anything to do with her step-family at all. In fact, she only ever made passing reference to her own grandparents and aunties, so I don't know much about that side of the family, or where any existing relatives would be now. She and her mother did continue to have a relationship until my grandmother passed away from cancer when she was in her late fifties. Despite her unpredictable and sometimes violent behaviour towards her, my mother would always maintain that her mother loved her.

In all honesty, I constantly wondered about this aspect of our relationship because I was never told that I was loved and, in view of my mother's behaviour towards me, I doubted that she even liked me. Her disciplinary methods programmed me to believe that other people didn't like me either.

I learnt, from a very young age, that affection had to be earned. If I was scared of anything, I was told not to be silly. If I needed a hug or a cuddle, she told me I was too big for that sort of thing.

If I didn't agree with her way, I was told that I was the one in the wrong.

It felt as if when I did things, I had done everything wrong. Equally, if I didn't do something, then I should have done. This led to a habit of self-loathing and these subconscious realisations gradually became my default settings which took up permanent residence.

As a result of this subliminal activity, I grew up with a warped view of the world, people, and relationships. I hadn't learnt what the rules were as regards integrating socially with other people because the rules would change on a daily basis for me, depending on what mood my mother was in.

My dad was born in Widnes, Cheshire. His dad and one of his older brothers worked on the railways as engineers. They had all been brought up in a very strict Brethren environment, and in those times, it had been the practice for the men to sit in the pews on one side of the Gospel Hall building and for the women to sit in the pews on the other side. The women were not encouraged to speak during the services.

My dad was told that his mother was of a delicate constitution and struggled to look after him, so he was sent to live with his sister, who was 18 years older than him. He was brought up with his nieces and nephews who were nearer to his age than his sister was and his own mum died when he was in his early teens.

My dad never really spoke of his childhood but a few years after he died, I met one of my cousins, and she told me that my dad had had a very difficult life, but he never discussed it with anyone.

The rest of my dad's family were all lovely, gentle, Christian folk, although there must have been domestic difficulties in their younger days because one of my dad's older brothers ran away from home, aged fourteen, lied about his age, and joined the navy.

If my memory serves me right, that happened before my dad was born in 1929, and he didn't meet that brother until a lot later in life. They had corresponded intermittently because his brother had settled in Australia many years before and had married and raised a family there.

I grew up knowing I had uncles, aunties, and an enormous number of cousins and second cousins but I only saw a very few members of my family on a very few occasions. I have never seen or heard about the vast majority of my family members who are scattered all over the world.

'Family' to me was made up of total strangers and if I did ever see any of them, it was a formal occasion where I had to get dressed up in my best clothes, drink my tea nicely out of a china cup, and speak when I was spoken to. I actually liked the ones I did get to meet, but I never got the chance to have a relationship with any of them.

My dad was born with a heart defect, involving his aortic valve, which was deformed and incompetent. His parents were told that he must never exert himself or play football or other sports, and it was unlikely he would live beyond twenty-one years old.

I assume that is why my dad did not go to work on the railways with the rest of his family, which would have been a very physical job, but went to work instead at the Clarks shoe factory in Blackpool after he left school, aged fourteen. He may have started as a machinist at the shoe factory because he was very capable of sewing leather into any shape or form. He would re-upholster seat covers and replace chair arm covers with carefully measured and designed pieces of leather, which he would confidently sew up on the very hefty, almost industrial, bad tempered Bernina sewing machine that belonged, strictly speaking, to my mother. This machine was the most temperamental thing you could ever wish to work with and it had bad days and worse days. My dad could usually coax it into compliance though and whatever he produced from this grumpy, metal contraption always came out perfectly and fit exactly.

He had gone on to become a shoe designer at Clarks. He would always inspect any shoes I bought when I was a teenager, or later for my own children, and usually pronounce them to be of inferior quality and 'not like the ones that were made in my day'.

He could do anything with his hands and had such a creative mind. He could even draw and paint, but rarely had the time to indulge that particular talent.

I loved my dad but he was hardly ever at home. When I was very young he became a sales rep for various companies, so he travelled long distances but, presumably, earned more money than working in a factory. I do remember going with him on a few occasions during the school holidays, though. I enjoyed those days. I learnt all the makes and types of cars on the road and where all the number plate suffixes came from. I would happily sit in the car with a book whilst he went into the company to do business, then he would come back, and we would drive to the next company, listening to Listen With Mother on Radio 4 at lunchtime. I think the car radio was mainly on Radio 3, so I developed quite an affinity for classical music.

He was a very gifted musician and was the church organist and choir leader. He went on to become Head of Music at a local school after he made a career change in his forties. He was always doodling on manuscript paper or designing something that he would make out of scraps, and he had lots of woodworking tools in the garden shed.

Despite the gloomy predictions of the doctors in his youth, my dad was active and capable, and lived long past twenty-one. He loved to swim and every time we went up to the Lake District, he would grab the chance to get into one lake or another and swim as far as he could.

There was always an annual church camping event on what used to be the Whitsun Tide weekend at the end of May. There would probably be 30 or 40 tents and related equipment transported from Preston to Grasmere on the Friday afternoon of the holiday and all the bottoms of these relatively small cars would be three inches off the ground under the weight of all that was necessary to sustain life for the next three or four days. Every car would have a roof rack, the packing of which would result in many fraught exchanges of words and heated arguments, or at least it did in our house.

My dad would carefully lay the enormous waterproof tarpaulin over the roof rack and pack all the suitcases, camp beds, camping chairs, table, double gas stove complete with gas bottles, water containers, airbed pump, washing up bowl, tent and groundsheet, mallet and tent pegs, and anything else that would fit up there, then carefully fold over all the corners of the tarpaulin so everything was covered. The whole lumpy bundle would then be secured by round, striped, stretchy luggage straps that had springs and hooks on the ends, which clamped everything down and attached neatly to the bars of the roof rack.

Anything that had to be kept dry, in the event of a rainy journey, had to be packed inside the car. So the airbeds, sleeping bags, towels, blankets, and pillows took priority over us kids, and were laid carefully along the width of the back seat. We were then positioned equally carefully on top of this considerable depth of soft furnishings and told to keep absolutely still for the duration of the journey, so as not to disturb or dirty anything. The food would be packed into the tiny car boot and all this activity invariably happened to the accompaniment of my mother's voice, stating 'I don't want that there,' and 'Be careful with that,' and 'No, that has to go somewhere else,' and 'Why are you doing it like that?' whilst my poor father sweated and heaved as per instructions.

Eventually we would set off, completely frazzled, with everyone's nerves hanging out the windows, and my mother still muttering in the front seat about things never being done correctly.

It would probably take a couple of hours to get there because, although the M6 had been built, the road into the Lake District was narrow and congested. The cars that we had then were old and could barely be relied upon to get themselves to and fro, much less when they were full of people, plus a loaded roof rack.

By the time we got to the field at Grasmere that was rented to the Church for the holiday period, we were all tired and hungry, but, before anyone could eat, the tent had to be erected.

The erection of a six-berth frame tent was not for the faint-hearted, so it involved a good deal of mutterings and trapped fingers. Everyone helped each other, generally, and as soon as there was a flat surface, clear of tent pegs, guy ropes, and folk waving their arms about, the gas stoves were lit, the cans were opened and the process of food preparation would begin. The smell of other people's food cooking in the open air and the distant sound of the clunking of cutlery on a camping table has always been an evocative experience and always makes me think affectionately of Grasmere, even now.

The inevitable consequence of nature taking its course after these al fresco meals was not one to be remembered with fondness, however.

The field that we rented was very short of modern conveniences. It was set on a very steep incline, the farm gate entrance being at the top of the hill with the field sloping down to the shores of Grasmere Lake. When I think about it, I am amazed that any of the cars we took in those days ever had the capability or energy to get off that field, especially if it was wet. The tents were all gathered together near the lake shore. Beautiful and tranquil though it was, that meant that calls of nature had to be answered at the very top of the hill.

It was quite a hike up to the top and not very discreet, because we would be clutching our toilet roll, so everyone knew who was on a mission. The reward for the steep climb was the vision of a corrugated tin roof which more or less covered a dilapidated stable-type building with a rotting wooden door which, for some reason, had random holes in. Once inside, we were greeted by a wooden seat running along the width of the shed, which had two holes cut out, side by side.

Now, to see one hole cut out was bad enough, but to see two holes was nothing short of alarming. It has always remained a point of morbid curiosity to me why anyone, however desperate, would want to share that malodourous, personal space with another person, no matter how well you knew them.

The smell of chemical toilet treatment was all-pervading and I assume that everything evacuated was directed into receptacles under the shed. I can't recall ever having the desire to investigate that particular mystery as I was quite happy to leave that end of the process to someone else.

The main concern of an anticipated trip to this shed would be to remember to bring your own toilet paper. If you impetuously decided to pay a visit whilst you were already at the top of the hill on other business, you would have to suffer the abhorrence of having to use the materials supplied by the management, namely, torn up pieces of newspaper, threaded on to a string and hung from a nail on the wall. There were no handwashing facilities, other than an outside cold water tap, fixed to a nearby building. This cold water tap also served as the water supply for the campers who had to lug their 25-gallon containers up the hill, fill them with water and rapidly learn the art of going back down the hill without gravitational forces taking the water container down first, with the camper manfully hanging on, a half-step behind.

Once safely down and back in the vicinity of the tent, this water was used for cooking, washing, and cleaning. Any hot water required had to be boiled in the tiny whistling kettle on the equally tiny camping stove. All washing up of dishes was done in a washing up bowl and the wastewater was then thrown onto the grass, away from your own tent, and, hopefully, not too near anyone else's. Any rubbish that accumulated had to be taken back up the hill to the dustbin which was thoughtfully provided.

If you wanted a bath or shower, you would have to wait until you went home. That was too much of a luxury for proper camping. Come to think of it, that was probably why everyone was so keen to swim every day.

There is an island in the middle of Grasmere Lake and I remember, on one camping trip, my dad decided that he was going to swim out to this island. Although it didn't look very far, it was a lot further away than someone with a dodgy heart, who didn't do regular exercise, who was not supposed to live past twenty-one, should have been considering as a destination to swim to. The more he thought about it and the more he discussed it with the other, equally unfit, normally office-based people on the camp, the grander his ideas became.

So, one morning after breakfast, my dad set off, into a cold lake, in May, with a few other men who thought they would also give it a go. However, my dad, wanting to go one better, decided to do the swim with my sister, who was probably aged around eleven or twelve at the time, perched on his shoulders.

I don't know whether the planning strategies of this expedition had included a return journey but, of course, that was also required, so after a short rest on the island, they all had to swim back. This time, my sister had to travel under her own steam. I don't recall him doing it again.

CHAPTER 4

Sing a Song

*When I taught myself to play the guitar
whilst singing along*

One feature of my childhood I do remember with affection was the little shop down the road which we called The Cabin. In truth, I think it was just set up in somebody's garage but it was a magical place where I spent my threepenny bit pocket money on Sherbet Dabs, Flying Saucers, Black Jacks or Fruit Salads, which were 4 for a penny (old money), Chewing Nuts, which were small spheres of chocolate coated caramels, and any amount of other old fashioned loose sweets which were sold by the quarter pound, dispensed out of big, glass jars, weighed out on brass scales then emptied into white paper bags. I suppose they may have sold other household essentials but those items didn't interest me then. When we moved up to the other end of Whitefield Road, it was nearer to go to the Howick Cross row of purpose-built shops, but that entailed crossing the busy Liverpool Road and the shops did not have such a magical appeal and sold a lot of prepacked sweets.

Negotiating the busy main road to get to the shops involved getting across halfway at a time. I remember, many a time, standing at the bollard in the middle of the road waiting to cross, dressed in the fashion of the day, and getting plenty of car horns tooting at me. In those days, when I was a teenager and had long legs worth showing off, I wore very, very short purple satin, bibbed hotpants. They were the height of fashion and I even went out in the evenings wearing them, teamed with knee high, leather boots.

*** That's at least one of my children rocking in a corner with their eyes shut tight and their ears covered, *la-la-la*-ing to block out the image! ***

The mini skirt was also the thing to wear in the late 60s and early 70s, and I owned a leather one, amongst others. This fairly immodest garment prompted the invention of tights for women as an alternative for the standard stockings that we were used to. It was unheard of for females of any age to go out with uncovered legs. Even answering your own front door with no hosiery on was considered slightly shocking, so a substitute had to be found, but I seem to remember the transition of getting used to these new-fangled tights was somewhat traumatic.

My aforementioned long legs didn't fit happily into these novel garments. The tights only came in one size and were expensive. The rest of my teenage years were spent hobbling around in some discomfort, owing to the fact that the crotch of these wretched things always ended up nearer my knees than where it was intended to be. Consequently, they were always splitting at the seams due to the extra strain they were under and they swallowed up a good proportion of the wages I earned from my Saturday jobs.

They were also 'run-resist', which just meant they didn't ladder. This was great if you didn't mind the gaping hole that appeared instead of a ladder. Many a bottle of clear nail varnish was utilised to dab on tiny holes to prevent them from getting more noticeable but it did mean very careful extrication of one's legs at bedtime when trying to peel off the nylon tubes that were now welded to one's skin with dried on nail varnish.

The other hot tip I can pass on is that if you had very long blonde hair, as I did, you could use a single hair, threaded into a fine sewing needle, then sew up the hole that way. You needed eyes like a sparrow hawk's, but it worked.

Our Deputy Headmistress at my secondary school thoroughly disapproved of mini skirts and tights. I think she had taken their invention as a personal affront and as a consequence, this disciplinarian was on a constant mission to banish such abominable things from her school, or at least register her objections to anybody wearing them. She sent out letters to all the girls' parents, telling them during exactly which school half-terms their daughters could wear socks in and when they had to change back and resume wearing stockings. She instructed the mothers to impress on their girls that they may *not* wear short skirts to school and that the tops of their stockings may not be displayed, nor should there be any holes or ladders in their hosiery. My mother did not take kindly to being instructed by anybody as to what her daughter should be doing or not doing, but she did convey the message to me in a begrudging sort of way, because she was, not unsurprisingly on this occasion, of the same opinion as the Deputy Head, apart from the bit about not having ladders or holes. She was in full favour of mended stockings, especially if they were mine, because school uniform was part of her financial outlay, which she liked to keep to a minimum.

So determined, was our Deputy Headmistress that her word would be implemented, she used to carry out spot checks on the girls during the lunchtime break. She would walk up quietly behind a group of nattering girls and instruct us all to kneel down. She then got out the tape measure that she had taken to carrying around with her and measure the distance between the bottom of our skirt hem and the floor. If the measurement was more than an inch, we would get lines to do as punishment. She wasn't at all fazed by how ridiculous she looked, grovelling around, just above the ground, peering at her tape measure to try to catch us out. Of course, she did catch us out, with alarming regularity. Our skirts had always started the day at the lawful length before we left the house, but somewhere on the journey between home and school, we had been busy turning the waistband over and over, thereby reducing the length of our skirts to a more fashionable dimension. If we kept alert and saw the dreaded Deputy heading our way, we frantically unrolled our waistbands at a furious pace, which must have been a comical sight to witness, and she wasn't as daft as we thought she was, hence her propensity to creep up behind people.

It was around this time that I decided I would like to learn to play the guitar. I was already having violin lessons on a weekly basis from a peripatetic teacher who came into school at lunchtimes, but it is a tad difficult singing along when you have an instrument thrust under your chin. There was no internet or YouTube to learn alongside, but there was Ralph McTell.

For the younger ones amongst you, Ralph McTell is a singer/songwriter who wrote 'Streets of London', which appeared first on an album, then was later released as a single. The attraction of this particular song was that it contained all the basic chords needed in order to learn to play the guitar. I invested in a book of chords, purchased from the music shop in town, and set about trying to decipher the foreign charts with dots on, and learning where to put my fingers to make the chord shapes.

I suffered for my art. To be fair, so did anyone else within a 200-yard vicinity of my musical development, who had to listen to screeches of horsehair on catgut disguised as violin practice and

Streets of London a thousand times a day whilst I fought with disjointed and jerky chord progressions. My fingers bled with the effort of getting my digits trained to position themselves promptly and accurately on the nylon guitar strings. My violin teacher was none too pleased when I started showing up for lessons with finger ends that were in shreds and gradually forming hard callouses.

Nevertheless, I persevered, learnt a lot more chords, and became proficient enough on my acoustic guitar to be able to accompany myself when I sang regularly at church. My main secular musical influence at that time (apart from Val Doonican singing Paddy McGinty's Goat) were The Carpenters and I would spend all my free time playing my LP vinyl records over and over again, trying to emulate Karen Carpenter's mellifluous tones. Hence, my homage to their songs in my chapter titles.

Decimalisation had landed on us in February 1971, and we had had much preparation for it at school. I was working in the school tuck shop at the time, so I had been specifically trained in the new coinage, known as new pence.

The existing money that we grew up with was:

Farthing worth ¼ d, (still used until 1960)

½ Penny or ½ d, pronounced *hayp-ny*

Penny or 1d

Threepenny Bit, pronounced *threp-ny* bit, worth 3d

Sixpence, worth 6d

Shilling or 1s

Florin, worth 2s

Half Crown, worth 2s 6d or 2/6

10 Shilling Note

£1 Note

Anything of greater value than that did not concern us kids, as we

never saw anything else until we started full-time, paid employment.
There were,
4 x Farthings in 1d, 960 in £1
3d in a 3d bit, 80 in £1
6d in a Sixpence, 40 in £1
12d in 1s, 240 in £1
20 x Shillings in £1
10 x Florins in £1
8 x Half Crowns in £1
2 x 10/- Notes in £1

It was quite straightforward, really. I can't think why they wanted
to change it.

Our young brains had already got to grips with such sums as these
every day:

£	s	d
4	18	7
+ 2	9	6 ½
= £7	8s	1 ½ d

When decimalisation came in, we now had 100 new pence in a
pound.
How hard could it be to divide everything up by 100?
You just had to do the conversion.
The old 10/- note was now 50p
The old florin was 2/-, now 10p
The old 1/- was now 5p
The 6d was now 2 ½ p
The 3d was now 1p, 1 ½ p or 2p depending on the shopkeeper

The 1d was now ½ p and, of course, everything went up in cost so it could be rounded up conveniently.

So... £2/11/6d + 19/4d used to add up to £3 10s 10d. Now it added up to £3 and 54 new pence or thereabouts.

You had to do all that adding up and converting whilst there was a queue of 30 shouting kids waiting at the tuck shop for Mars bars during a 10-minute break between lessons.

In your head. Without a calculator. Simple.

It took years for the monetary system to go completely decimal. There were some businesses, such as market stalls and petrol garages, which simply refused to change or had both currencies running side by side for a long time. Folk were allowed to make the change at their own pace so it was incredibly confusing and you had to constantly check that you weren't being ripped off by traders whose conversion tactics were loaded in their favour.

One of the first Saturday jobs I had was down the road in the newly built Mace convenience store. I think I would be around fourteen years old and I distinctly remember the smell of the storeroom behind the shop which was a combination of disinfectant and cheese. My main role was to stack shelves but I have vague recollections of playing with the cheese cutter and cooked meat slicer. Whether I did that legally or not, we won't dwell on.

I moved on to work at a local petrol station where my dad was working part time, due to the fact that he had decided on a career change when he was in his forties, and went to do his teacher training as a mature student. It was a 24-hour garage, and he would often do the night shift to earn some money whilst he was training during the day. I wasn't as daft, so I opted for the Saturday hours. In those days, there was no such thing as self-service so every customer was served with either 3-star, 4-star or, if you were really rich, 5-star petrol. I think the price was around 37 new pence per gallon.

I ultimately progressed from serving petrol, derv and 2-stroke and checking folks' oil via dipsticks, and trying to remove red hot car radiator covers without removing facial skin in the ensuing angry steam, to much more genteel and civilised occupations.

I used to babysit for a couple who lived in the area and had several children. How those kids had the energy to function was a mystery because they never were keen on sleep. I used to give up on them and left them to wreak havoc in their bedroom whilst I ate the very nice supper that was always provided for me.

At Christmas time, the lady of the house said she had left me something to make a lovely festive drink with. She told me to put a small amount from the bottle on the kitchen counter into a glass, then top it up with lemonade. I followed her instructions whilst reading the label on the unfamiliar bottle, which was, literally, double Dutch to me. I wasn't over impressed with the taste but I didn't want to appear rude when she later asked me if I had liked it.

It transpired that the young girl temporarily in charge of her beloved offspring had been instructed to make herself a Snowball. The bottle with the funny label on was the Advocaat.

Up to then, I'd lived a sheltered life. Now, I'd been persuaded to take the first step on the road to alcohol addiction. Well, maybe that was a slight exaggeration.

A few months down the line, when the next baby's arrival was imminent, I was told by the couple that they would not be requiring my services anymore, but their friends, who lived nearby, needed a babysitter.

The lovely lady I worked for did not actually say I could not be trusted with a small baby, but that was surely what she meant. After all, what doting parent would want to trust a teenager, who unknowingly experimented with alcohol whilst on duty, with their new bundle of joy?

It turned out that the kids over the road had been coached in the fine art of winding up babysitters by the little cherubs who were now my former clients. The parents were super people but I only stayed a few months in that job. The quality of the suppers was not quite up to the standard to which I had become accustomed, but I did get to watch colour television for the first time on my Saturday night sittings.

I wish to state, for the record, that I remained entirely sober for the duration of that employ.

Over the next two or three years I had a couple of jobs in confectioner's shops in Preston town centre. There, I served luscious cakes in white, cardboard, ready-to-assemble boxes so the icing or cream topping wouldn't squash, and freshly made sandwiches or fresh loaves of bread in crisp, white paper bags. I got to do that thing that we all practised as children where you twisted the corners of the bag round in mid-air whilst keeping everything flat and the right way up. I also was allowed to play with the cash till. No credit or debit cards, just cash and all the workings out in our heads. You could write the amounts on the empty paper bag if it was a long order, and then add it up like we were taught at school. I had my pick of the café options for my lunch every day during the school summer holidays and generally enjoyed myself a lot more there than working with smelly petrol.

I was offered a job as full-time manageress of the St Anne's branch of Kenyon's Confectioners where I worked during my last holidays after college had finished. Whilst I really enjoyed the job, I had always set my heart on doing my SRN nurse training, so I reluctantly declined the Supervisor's offer.

CHAPTER 5

Close to You

Where romance and courtship began

By the time I had gained employment in Preston town centre, I was at college. I had always wanted to be a nurse, as far back as I could think, so when I left Secondary School, I decided to go on to Sixth Form College. I didn't actually need A Levels to gain a place in a nursing school as I was already in possession of five O Levels and several CSEs, but in order to guarantee getting a place in a good hospital I thought I would spend the next couple of years developing my education as much as I could, until I was old enough to start my nurse training.

I studied English Literature, Music, and Domestic Science at A Level, and Human Biology, which I hadn't been able to do at school, and General Studies at O Level. These subjects were all studied in great depth and most of them have proved to stand me in good stead for the occupations I had later on in life. There were very few free periods allowed as a lot of lesson time was devoted to each subject.

My English teacher found out I could sing and play the guitar, so she would instruct me to track down Shakespearean ballads, learn them, and sing them in the class whenever one came up in the section of text we were studying. Bearing in mind that this was in the days before the internet, I would make a regular nuisance of myself in the Preston Harris Library, pestering the librarians to locate old manuscripts of these long forgotten songs (usually with good reason) so I could borrow them, learn the wretched things and sing them to the class next time they were required. I never got any extra marks for all this extracurricular activity, just extra embarrassment at being made to do all this in front of classmates who were probably no more enthused by Shakespeare than I was, whether it was sung or spoken. I seem to remember making up a good proportion of the tunes if I couldn't locate the original music. But, when you've heard one Shakespearean ballad, you've heard them all, so no one noticed.

I also ran the Rhythm and Blues Club which was held monthly in college rooms in Winckley Square in town *in the evenings!* This was my teenage rebellion. I got to sing worldly songs that were in the Hit Parade in front of people! My parents were not happy as I was doing things other than church activities and who knows where it could have led? Clearly, I was heading down a slippery slope, and to them it was only a matter of time before I became completely heathen. I was given a stern talking to and made to see the error of my ways, so I gave it up. But not before I had starred in a couple of Gilbert & Sullivan operas, The Gondoliers and The Pirates of Penzance, which were, again, performed in the evening, in the centre of Preston.

The Domestic Science course at college was sold to me under the guise of Advanced Level of Food Preparation, which I assumed, and hoped, was along the lines of learning to ice and decorate wedding cakes and the like. That's why I turned up.

It was all too late when I realised I had been duped. I was expected to study The Family in Society, which involved the Industrial Revolution and the Science of Food. Now, although both these subjects fascinate me now, at that time I was horrified. It was basically History and Chemistry, both subjects that I had skilfully avoided like the plague at school, yet here they expected me to study them at A Level. I was not thrilled. The only bit of that course I enjoyed was the triple lesson of actual cooking which took place on Wednesday afternoons.

I would gather every last ingredient, despite my mother telling me that such-and-such wasn't available, so I would have to use such-and-such instead—items that would have changed the original recipes into something which would have been totally unrelated—and I even had to provide such minutiae as salt and pepper, ingredients which would have been already in the classroom kitchen, back in my school days.

I would trundle all my bags, bowls and equipment on the two buses necessary to transport me from Penwortham to Preston Bus Station, then out again to Moor Park Avenue in Preston. The Sixth Form College was a newly created institution, combining the buildings of Preston Boy's Grammar School, situated at the Deepdale Road end of Moor Park Avenue, and the Preston Park School for Girls, which was at the Garstang Road end. There were still the last of the pupils attending these schools in their original form when we started at college so it was a new enterprise for all concerned.

We thought we were the bee's knees when we scorned the leather satchels of our school days and purchased briefcases to use at college, to keep all our important foolscap-sized papers nice and flat. These briefcases worked quite well, although you had to be creative with the shape of your sandwiches and choice of lunchbox in order to make everything flat enough to actually fit inside the posh briefcase, but when it came to juggling a wicker basket full of breakable, spillable food items, plus other bags as well as said briefcase, and having a hand free to fish out the correct change for the bus fare, the journey to and from college every Wednesday became rather fraught. It was always a lottery as to whether the carefully prepared creation of Advanced Food got home in a presentable and still-edible condition.

It was at Sixth Form College that Philip and I met. He was based at the Grammar School end of Moor Park, mainly studying Sciences, and I was based at the Park School end, trying to avoid studying Sciences and stay in my comfort zone of English and Music. There were weekly lunchtime Christian Union meetings in a room at the Park School which I would turn up to, and he would drive down to. At that time, Philip was in possession of a Suzuki motorbike, which was the most efficient way of getting him from the nether reaches of Woodplumpton, where buses were few and far between, to college every day. His motorbike also proved to be the most efficient way of getting himself back home in the middle of the day at lunchtimes, or when he was bunking off college when he had free periods or when he should have been in games lessons. However, when it was the CU lunchtime, he stayed at college and made the trip down the avenue, always wearing his light brown, knee length, belted, faux leather coat, with the black faux fur collar plus regulation crash helmet, to attend.

After a while, he started to come down to the Park School Common Room nearly every lunchtime, armed with his sandwiches, always made from cottage cheese on substantial, round slices of white Big T Milk Roll bread, and partake of the coffee that was available there. I just assumed that the coffee at the Park School was superior to the coffee at the Grammar School.

It was freshly made by a tiny lady with red hair poking out from under her white catering hat, who disappeared behind vast clouds of white-hot steam which gushed out from the massive stainless steel machine every time she prepared another metal jugful of lava-like coffee. You could be forgiven for thinking The Royal

Scotsman steam engine had screeched to an abrupt halt outside the common room window, such was the racket that ensued. The dark brown liquid was served in white Pyrex cups and remained at a searing temperature for the duration of the lunch break. No one else would dare attempt to actually drink the stuff without giving it at least ten minutes to stop bubbling, but Philip would nonchalantly take mouthfuls in between his bites of sandwich and never flinch. I found it morbidly fascinating.

Having conversations around this shrieking, steaming contraption in the background was challenging, but we must have made some sort of connection and managed a level of communication because he subsequently invited me to his church bonfire in November 1973. This event was to prove the start of a very long-term relationship.

I have to say, our first date did not start well.

Philip had arranged to borrow his mum's car on that Saturday evening and was prepared to make the long trek across Preston to pick me up from Penwortham and take me to the bonfire which was being held in a field next to Crown Lane Church in Bartle.

I had looked forward to it all week and had got myself dolled up and dressed in my finery, or as fine as you can get for a date in a field, and went down to answer the knock which came on the door at the appointed time.

It wasn't Philip. It was one of his friends who arrived with two more of his friends, in his friend's car.

Now, it wasn't what you think. I know no self-respecting female with the slightest sense of self-preservation would have willingly got into a car with three young men, but I did.

I did actually know these lads who were Philip's friends because I had attended his church on other occasions. Let's just say I'd had reason to accompany another young man a few months previously, who also went to that church, and so I had got to know folk.

So, instead of the anticipated position in the front seat, being chauffeured to my first date and feeling special, I was ungallantly squeezed into the back seat, where I learnt the reason why my future husband had sent emissaries instead of picking me up in person.

Apparently, Philip had been riding his motorbike that lunchtime, having been given time off from his Saturday job, working on his uncle's farm, to go home for his lunch. According to his uncle's telling of the tale later, Philip's mind hadn't been on what he was doing because some woman was distracting his thoughts, and it was on his return to work that he managed to collide with the 2-hourly service double decker bus on a particularly tight corner in Woodplumpton village. This corner was not only tight but was also bordered by a singularly solid stone wall that ran along the front of a garden. With no room to swerve, he made spectacular contact, scraping down the entire length of the bus with his leg and sustained a bit of a graze, a split-second before the rest of him hit the ground in a heap.

When I say 'a bit of a graze', I may be understating ever so slightly. He spent the rest of the afternoon in A & E having his injuries assessed and sutures inserted where necessary. His particularly bony knee, which, up until that day, had been one of a matching pair, had suffered the worst consequence of the impact and was now sewn together to stop bits falling off and, more importantly, it was scarred for life. The whole incident could have ended so differently and it's such a good job that he didn't subsequently have need of the church graveyard, which stood exactly opposite to the point where he had smashed into the bus.

I must say, as excuses go for being stood up, I suppose it wasn't bad.

However, I wasn't stood up after all. Such was his determination to see the bonfire and fireworks, he had raised himself from his settee of pain, borrowed a walking stick, and persuaded his mother to drive him to the venue. And so he materialised on the field through the smoky darkness that evening and greeted me with a rather wry smile. I thought it only right, as a prospective nurse, that I should assist him and prop him up on the other side to his walking stick. The fact that we were soon holding hands was purely coincidental and clinically necessary.

I spent the rest of the evening being shamelessly stared at by all Philip's younger cousins and there was a lot of giggling with heads together and comments behind cupped hands as they followed us around.

I can't remember whether the fireworks were any good, but I am certain that, if Philip's mum had known where that lift she gave him to the bonfire was going to lead, she would have strapped him down to the settee and 'grazed' his other knee, so he would be grounded for the next six months.

CHAPTER 6

Hurting Each Other

*The painful recall of extracting rubber
bands from long hair*

I had been brought up in the Pentecostal church in Preston, where my dad was the organist and choirmaster. I still attended there when I met Philip and although our respective churches were in very different locations there were quite strict rules in both places of worship, and we both had had a fairly conservative upbringing.

The preachers, pastors, and leadership at his rural chapel and my town centre church were second to none. They were all, without exception, strong, dependable, faithful, Godly people who preached Bible truths at every service. I had been brought up through the Sunday School, with loving, caring women who taught every child scripture passages which set them up for life. No one who attended either of those churches in any capacity was ever left in any doubt about the Gospel and how to apply it to their lives.

There was, however a rule at North Road Pentecostal Church that could never be broken. The ladies were *required* to wear hats. Indeed, there were some other Pentecostal churches that we visited as youth groups, where, if we turned up without hats, the girls were often given headscarves to wear for the duration of the service. I have to admit, until the age of seventeen, when I went off the rails and started to go to the *Free Methodist Church in the company of a young man*, I accepted and quite liked the wearing of hats.

As children, it was tradition that we got a new outfit at Easter, usually with a new straw, or lightweight hat for summer, which was replaced with a more substantial one in autumn, to cope with winter weather.

The hats we wore kept up with the fashion of the day and most were quite similar in style, just different colours and slight variations, but they posed a bit of a problem.

Such was the design of the old church building that the toilets, which boasted a mirror on the wall, were located right around the back of the car park and generally had to be accessed by going outside. Naturally, this was of no use whatsoever to us ladies who were expected to be turned out in a pristine manner, and we always got blown to bits on our return journey from 'spending a penny', as it was discreetly termed. The problem was rectified by the thoughtful provision of a hat room located just inside the main church entrance. This consisted of an area under the stairs, fitted with a single light bulb, perfectly positioned to blind you in one eye, and the tiniest mirror you could imagine, screwed into the crumbling plaster at approximately chest height. There was a shelf fixed to the entire width, which supported a huge cardboard box containing—yes, hats!

There was always a spare hat available for any lady turning up to church and feeling awkward because she was hatless. She would be shaken warmly by the hand and swiftly directed to the salubrious hat room, where she would be invited to take her pick and borrow a hat for the duration of the service. I'm not sure the kind invitations to wear a second-hand hat of dubious origin were always fully appreciated, but, the offer was there.

This facility was barely adequate when the hat of the day was an adorable, satin-lined fur hood (many colours were available) with leather strings to which fur pompoms were attached, because all you had to do was tie the string in a bow and pull until the pompoms came together to sit snugly under your chin, thus leaving no hair on view to bother about or comb. However, it wasn't long before the wide-brimmed, floppy, felt hat became *de rigueur*. Mine was yellow and went very well with my knee length, black leather, platform-soled boots, and my much loved purple wool maxi length coat, or least it was considered to, back in the 70s.

The trouble was, trying to get my aforementioned long legs, now extended somewhat by the platform soles and heels I was wearing, along with the rest of me, topped with a high-domed, wide-brimmed floppy hat—which could compromise your field of vision if it wasn't arranged just right—into the bespoke but very snug, triangular space became a bit of an issue. The only way to assess whether my up-to-the-minute fashion accessory was perched at *exactly* the right angle was to perform a sort of bob-like curtsy and contort myself diagonally, so I could see half a head at a time.

When the hat was considered fit enough to be seen in public, I turned my attention to the long, flowing, blonde locks cascading down from underneath my perfectly positioned brim, to gently coax my hair to create just the perfect effect for maximum impact.

Sounds impressive, doesn't it?

The truth was, my hair did make an impact but not the type I had intended. I let my hair grow long as my mother wouldn't pay hairdresser prices to have it cut properly so it was a choice of long or pudding basin-style. It was actually a sea of split ends. Conditioner was not a feature of our bathroom, indeed I was lucky to find proper shampoo. The remnants of war rationing mentality lasted a long time in our house and my mother could not see why a good, cheap block of green household soap wouldn't serve for every cleaning process and that included bodies and hair more often than not.

I would wash my hair over the sink (no showers in those days) and use a jug to rinse as much soap scum out as possible. My hair would be towelled furiously, then, in a bid to tame the frizz which would always ensue not surprisingly, I would fasten it into a tight ponytail, which I then tucked under and used further bands to anchor everything down in some sort of stranglehold, so I could go to bed with it wet and wake up in the morning with smooth, sleek, perfectly formed waves.

That was the theory.

In reality, because I had had to use ordinary rubber bands since I did not possess any proper covered hair bobbles, the amount of pain involved and wrestling required to remove those tenacious pieces of elastic rendered my beautifully tamed hair into a mass of troubled, still-damp, straw-like strands, none of which wanted to sit side by side with their fellow strands. I permanently had the look of someone who had spent too much time on a high cliff, looking out to sea in a force ten gale. A lot of my spare time was spent trying to untangle tightly wrapped strands of long, blonde hair from off the rubber bands that caused so much carnage every week.

When I was taken to meet Philip's family, as was the next step in a serious relationship when you were 'going out' with someone in the 1970s, things did not go particularly well.

Philip's mother must have wondered what on earth had landed in her living room that Saturday, early on in our relationship. No one had ever entered her house before who had designs on her eldest son and suddenly, there was a young female—a townie, no less—and what is more, she was wearing make-up!

I had always had a particularly sensitive skin which was constantly in some state of eruption on my face. To try and tone down the angriness and in an attempt cover up the lumps and bumps, I always wore make-up. The foundation was, in my opinion, necessary, and the mascara wearing—well, it's what you did when you were 17.

Unfortunately though, I fear that was the first reason why I lost points, coupled with the threat of running off with her firstborn. Make-up was not always considered appropriate for nice Christian girls in that era and it cast uncertainties on whether my questionable habits might prove entirely suitable for the long haul, so to speak.

The second reason why there were concerns about my suitability addressed the subject of my choice of clothes. In the last twelve months, as well as being able to afford proper shampoo, at last, I had started to earn enough money to be able to choose what I wore and the availability of styles and colours of outfits in the mid-70s was eclectic, to say the least.

I had worn bright red trousers. They were less than subtle and, unbeknown to me, trousers on respectable young ladies were not considered entirely suitable either.

The only trousers that would have been acceptable were jodhpurs, and only then when worn in the close vicinity of an actual horse, which made them garments for practicality rather than a fashion choice.

His poor mother's silent gaze started at my platform soles and travelled slowly up the considerable length, as we have already established, of my legs which, although starting off modestly clad with flared bottoms, then degenerated into limbs attired with tight-fitting trousers of the high-waisted variety, into which was tucked an aptly-named, canary yellow, skinny ribbed jumper. I had not got an ounce of spare fat in those days and all the curves and bumps were in the right places, so, although I say it myself, my figure made the most of the close-fitting fashion garments of the era. Philip always seemed impressed by what I wore.

His mother, not so much.

CHAPTER 7

Please, Mister Postman

*The only period in our lives when we
wrote letters to each other*

Of course, as time went on, I grew to appreciate Philip's mum's apprehension about me—or anyone else, at that stage—coming into her family's life and disrupting the status quo. I was the pioneer daughter-in-law at the time, but over the years, we have become very close, and she is the best mother-in-law anyone could have. She has been there for me during many difficult times, and has moved in and run my household on several occasions, when necessary.

She had good reason to feel threatened when I came on the scene. Philip was the eldest of six children. His dad had suffered from kidney failure and had died when he was only just into his thirties, leaving a young widow and six children aged between 3 months and ten years old. Philip had to take on the role of being the man of the house and father-figure to his younger siblings, and he supported his mum in maintaining a good measure of stability and security. He would often come up behind one of the younger children when they were giving cheek to their mum and give them a swift clip around the ear—perfectly acceptable and indeed, encouraged in those days—and tell them not to be so cheeky. His mum relied on him heavily in many ways and as soon as he was old enough to pass his driving test, a lot of the ferrying of children and running-around jobs were transferred to him. It was not surprising then, that when I and my form-hugging trousers and jumper appeared, topped by all that make-up, and wanted to make claim to her right-hand man, she had grave misgivings.

I'll not deny it. It wasn't the smoothest of courtships. There was a lot of opposition to our relationship, especially as it was obvious it was heading towards marriage. We were both only seventeen and, although as an adult it is easier to look back and appreciate what difficulties would be caused when the family dynamic was disrupted by Philip leaving the family home, at the time it was hard to see the situation from any other viewpoint than our own.

As it was, we got engaged on the 20th of July 1974; he was eighteen and I was still seventeen years old. There was no marriage proposal, but we would wander round jeweller's shop windows on Saturday afternoons, trying to find something that looked the most impressive for the meagre amount of money we could afford to part with. It was my parents' 25th wedding anniversary that year, and they had planned a trip to South Africa to visit my sister and her family who lived there, and I was going with them. Philip was keen on us being engaged before I went, so I could show off the ring.

On this particular Saturday, we found a diamond ring that we liked and could afford, and a signet ring for Philip to wear, so we excitedly made the purchases. Philip had done the decent thing on a previous occasion and requested my dad's permission to marry me and, although Dad had readily agreed—anything to get me off his hands—he wasn't expecting the engagement to happen any time soon.

It's probably better to gloss over the reception we got from all concerned when we got back from town, proudly exhibiting our new rings. Suffice to say, the enthusiasm was less than we had hoped for. My dad went a very funny colour at the prospect of having to pay for the myriad hordes of Parkinson relatives at the wedding reception and my mother had plenty to say about who would or wouldn't be coming to the wedding. It was still hoped that we would come to our senses, even at that stage.

The plan to dazzle my sister with my ring very nearly went awry the following week, when I realised, after setting off for the airport, en route to our South African holiday, that I had washed my hands just before leaving the house and my sparkling gem was still sitting in splendid isolation on the kitchen windowsill. I made my dad turn the car around and let me go back for it. He was not best pleased, but he had learnt the wisdom of obeying his womenfolk the hard way.

My sister in South Africa was suitably impressed by my ring, and she was my ally because she had also endured family opposition and got married when she was very young. For the duration of the time we were apart, Philip and I wrote so many letters to each other and used up so many aerogrammes and airmail paper. It was the only way to keep in touch as there were no email or text facilities and telephone calls were prohibitively expensive. We certainly kept the postman busy. By the time I returned home, I'm sure I would have been qualified for a job in Bletchley Park. Philip's handwriting was so small and barely decipherable, it could have been some sort of cryptic code.

We spent most of our leisure time at Crown Lane Church, where the youth group was active and thriving and consisted mainly of Philip's many cousins. His aunties and uncles who attended this church were staunch believers in church growth and in the years running up to this decade had supplemented the congregation magnificently in the form of biological contributions.

There was the youth activity on Friday night for the 9–12-year-olds where Philip was one of the leaders. With it being out in the country, there was no suitable bus service available, so most of the kids would be given a lift by one leader or another.

Now, this lift did not involve neatly seat-belted youngsters fitted correctly on the back seat of the car, oh no.

There would be at least three children on the front bench seat of his mum's Morris Oxford. He could easily squeeze six on the back seat—everyone had knees to sit on, after all—and there was a really roomy boot, which, if they didn't object too much to the smell of dried on, often-spilt liquid eggs and cow-mucked wellies, provided a comfortable, reclined position for a couple more kids.

If they could locate the button which operated the interior boot light and keep their finger pressed on it for the entire journey, they could have the light on as well. Not one child (or driver) was strapped in, but they were crammed in that tightly, no one was going anywhere anyway.

This economical form of transportation did let us down at times and the health and safety of the car occupants and the wisdom of the scheme was occasionally queried, albeit briefly.

We had done the usual shoehorning of children into the Morris Oxford on the way back from Sunday School one afternoon and arrived back home without incident. The boot lid was being lifted to release the youngest sibling from the boot, when a peculiar, agonised cry was emitted from within. In an effort to locate the reason for the noise, the boot lid was lifted faster but the noise got louder. I can't remember exactly who said what to whom in those couple of seconds but the boot lid was rapidly dropped back down whilst little brother removed his thumb from the hinge inside the boot.

The lid was raised again to reveal a grey-looking youngster who had a strange expression on his face. There was rather a lot of blood involved and I remember holding his arm aloft in an effort to reduce the flow of blood. I assume he was taken to hospital for repairs or maybe not. I would not have liked to have been the person explaining how the injury occurred.

His thumb survived on that occasion but, a few years later, the same brother had an altercation with a circular saw whilst he was slicing wood in a farm workshop. He spent many, many days in Wythenshawe Hospital near Manchester, having his completely detached thumb reattached and a badly severed hand painstakingly repaired by a very gifted microsurgeon. I can't help thinking he demonstrated a distinct disregard towards the value of some of his bodily parts and really should have paid more attention to keeping things attached.

The older end of the youth formed a group known as The Crown Lane Singers, and we spent many a Saturday evening travelling around the Fylde and into Yorkshire. Although we were all Lancashire lads and lassies, we weren't afraid to go over the border into Yorkshire. There was safety in numbers.

There must have been twenty-five to thirty members in this group of singers and musicians, and we had regular invitations to sing at all sorts of church events throughout the year. We frequently doubled the congregation when we all traipsed in and sat down. There were always magnificent suppers provided for us all afterwards. Even at small venues, there would be lines of tables in the kitchen or adjoining hall, which were weighted down with sandwiches, meat pies, quiches, cakes, fruit pies, trifle, cream cakes, etc., all of which were homemade by the ladies of the church.

We even had proper outfits to help make us look the part.

One colour combination that was agreed on was navy blue skirts for the girls and navy trousers for the boys, with navy polo neck silky tops for the girls, accessorised with a pale blue scarf and pale blue shirts for the lads. We girls obviously did our own shopping to ensure that we looked like we owned the clothes we were wearing, rather than having borrowed them from someone who was a different dress size to us. The lads sent an envoy into Preston town centre, tasked with purchasing pale blue shirts, which were all the same. The appointed personal shopper came back, feeling rather smug that he had sourced and purchased exactly the right shade of blue.

It was just a pity they were nylon. The boys all sweated and scratched their way through the summer months and didn't smell too good either. On the plus side, though, the shirts didn't need ironing. Another collective outfit idea was black skirts/trousers and pale green blouses/shirts and I distinctly remember, in late 1977, struggling to make my waistband fit, then extending it with large safety pins, then finally giving in to having to make a maternity pinafore out of black fabric, to accommodate my developing bump when I was expecting our first baby.

I also did a lot of solo singing and one of Philip's uncles would often ask us both to go with him when he preached. He was a very well-known Methodist preacher and spent most of his weekends visiting churches all over the area. I would sing and play my acoustic guitar and Philip would play the bass guitar to accompany me, always supposing there was an electrical socket available that he could plug his amplifier into. We played in tiny chapels, where the fruit and veg harvest festival displays were so extravagant we could barely access the pulpit; we played in hay barns, where all the seats were bales of straw and the cable extensions ran across the farmyard, so we could plug the amplifier in; we played on street corners, in big churches, small churches, church halls, house groups and anywhere else that would hold a gathering of people. I've even sung in the Guild Hall in Preston. I remember many a time singing a song, realising that I hadn't a clue what the next line was, and making up the words as I went along. I think I mostly got away with it.

These musical experiences were all much more informal than what I had been brought up with in my town centre church. On one occasion I was asked to go back and sing some solos at a service in my parents' church, quite some years after I had got married and moved to Crown Lane. The service went well, I sang my songs, remembered the words and got lots of approving looks as I sat down.

Nobody clapped in those days, though. It wasn't considered quite the thing to do in church. Afterwards, my dad came up and said, 'Yes, it was very nice.' (High praise indeed).

'But next time, you've got to wear a hat.'

'I haven't got a hat,' I said, stubbornly.

'You can borrow one of your mother's,' he said.

I didn't sing there again.

CHAPTER 8

I Won't Last A Day Without You

All things bedpan related

I left college after my A-Level exams and that was the summer I had spent working in cake shops. I started my student nurse training at Manchester Royal Infirmary in September 1974. It was as far as I could get away from home without it costing a fortune to travel back to spend time with Philip on my days off.

I had done my research about the various schools of nursing that I could have attended. You may think that I was being very thorough about what standard of teaching and clinical placements I could expect and what would be the best experiences I could gain during my training—but no.

My sole purpose to this in-depth research was to ascertain which hospital had the nicest uniform.

Times were changing as far as hospital uniforms were concerned and I didn't want to waste all those childhood imaginings of me gracefully and silently gliding up the ward, intent on cooling fevered brows and offering sips of water to those in need, doing my best Florence Nightingale impersonation. Bedpans, sputum pots, and vomit bowls hadn't featured large in my imaginings, I have to say. But, I was on a mission. I had caps to starch and aprons to swish. Lead on.

As well as being suitably positioned geographically, Manchester Royal turned out to be the winner in my best uniform search. They still had the traditional striped dresses with those little white, stretchy detachable cuffs, with white cotton, bibbed aprons that pinned on at the front, with long, elegant straps that fastened behind in a long bow, and proper starched caps. Sisters' caps even had a frill around the top, and I was looking forward to working up to achieving one of those. When I went for my interview, I couldn't take my eyes off the apparel I had coveted for so long. My dreams were about to come to fruition.

We were required to report to the Nurses Home on the Sunday, ready for the start of the training the following day. I had packed all the stuff I thought I might need for a couple of weeks into my parents' car. They had offered to take me to Manchester, probably to make sure I actually got there, and Philip came as well.

I had previously received all the documentation, which would have been laboriously, individually typed up by Matron's secretary, on an old-fashioned typewriter—no computers or word processors in those days—telling me what I would be letting myself in for, all the weird and wonderful immunisations that I must have had before I arrived, and a list of requirements that I had to purchase before I would be allowed through the hallowed gates of the Training School.

1 x pair Oxford-type, Brown Leather, Lace Up, Rubber Soled Shoes
4 x pairs 20 Denier Black Tights
1 x Watch, Pin-on type, with Second-Hand
1 x pair Blunt-ended Surgical Scissors
1 x Pen Torch with spare Batteries
1 x set Hairgrips, White
1 x set Ballpoint Pens with clips, Black, Blue, Red, Green

Please bring writing implements, rubber & ruler for school work.

Medium to long hair must be fastened back and must not touch the collar.

No piercings, tattoos, wrist watches, or items of jewellery are permitted. Plain wedding bands may be worn.

So far, so good. The tights and shoes would go very nicely with that lovely striped dress and the hair grips were for the starched cap. And so I arrived with anticipation.

After all the relatives had gone back home, later that first afternoon, it was a strange time and I felt completely abandoned.

The room I had been allocated was at the stair end of the corridor, next to the double fire doors, which banged every time anyone came through them, and it was a most peculiar shape. The door, which had a Yale lock and, I learnt, was determined to lock me out at every opportunity, touched the bed next to the wall when it opened. The width of the single bed plus the door made up the dimensions of the room at one end.

At the foot end of the bed, the wall changed direction and angled itself sharply towards the window, then finished at the window end with just enough room for a small wardrobe to be squeezed in. There was the tiniest hand wash basin on the other side of the window, plumbed into the opposite wall, and next to that was an old-fashioned dressing table with a large mirror attached. I had a long triangular shaped space measuring approximately six feet by ten feet, diminishing to four feet across the window wall, and that was to be my home for the next twelve months. It smelt old and musty and the twelve inches of carpet visible between my bed and the dressing table looked very dingy and tired.

The long, narrow kitchen was a couple of doors down the corridor and the two toilet cubicles and bathroom were positioned in the centre of the corridor.

Yes, that's right. Two toilets, one bathroom.

The corridor held ten bedrooms, which meant there was a fair chance, depending on shift patterns, that the requirements of the number of girls needing to use the toilet and bathroom at the same time far exceeded the availability of these very necessary facilities. The positive aspect to these archaic sanitary arrangements, though, was greatly improved by the fact that the bath was a Victorian claw-footed, cast iron affair, which was fixed centrally in the massive room which, I'm sure, was larger than my bedroom, and this bath was of chasm-like proportions. The ornate brass taps happily gushed forth as much hot water as was wanted and, if you were so inclined, you could sit up to your chest in your well-earned soak, such was the depth of the bath. Of course, the fact that every other exhausted body that had just finished a shift, was in need of the same restorative treatment and the neighbours were forming a queue outside the door, curtailed the length of the luxury somewhat, but if you picked your time right, you soon learnt how to get the maximum benefit.

Despite the misgivings I had about my room, I slept okay that night and was woken up the following morning by the brand new Baby Ben alarm clock that had been purchased as an absolute necessity for summoning me out of my deep sleeps. In those days, I could sleep on a washing line, and the Baby Ben was not named that for nothing. The domestic equivalent of its southern cousin, Big Ben, I like to think I provided a service to the whole corridor by rousing everyone with the ear-splitting ringing, whether they needed to be up at the same time as me, or not.

We all found our way downstairs to the Nurses Common Room, where we were greeted on that first day by our Sister Tutor. She was a lovely lady, not at all like the barking, bossy tyrant we might have expected her to be. She had a wonderful sense of humour, which helped with all the awkward bodily bits and functions we later had to learn about, but she was extremely thorough and demanded excellence. She managed to elicit the maximum effort and application from all her pupils, as time went on, but, in the first couple of hours of our acquaintance, she also managed to deliver a major disappointment.

After the statutory induction talk, the do's and don'ts, more don'ts and thou-shalt-nots, we all trouped down to the Uniform Supply Department.

This was it. The excitement was mounting. We all filled in the slips of paper, stating our dress sizes and waited whilst the assistant scurried to the back room to locate the necessary uniforms.

To say we felt let down was an understatement.

In the time lapse between our interviews and our induction date, the Board, in their wisdom, had decided to update and modernise the uniforms.

We removed the plastic wrapping off our plain green, short-sleeved, drip-dry shift dresses, with zip-up fronts, with waning enthusiasm.

True, there were white, detachable collars, but they could not make up for white, removable cuffs. Then, to add insult to injury, we were each handed three paper, yes, *paper* caps. They came as flat packs, and we were given instruction on how to fold the uninspiring shapes into the correct triangular requirement, and then fix them together with white plastic studs that were to be the bane of our lives from that moment on, as they were always getting lost.

The only redeeming feature of this modernised uniform was that we were still given a dark green, proper wool cape, which had a coloured satin lining and fastened by criss-crossing the attached ties around the body, from front to back.

We were sent back to our rooms to change into our new uniforms, work out how best to perch the bits of paper on our heads and make a plan as to which hairstyle would accommodate all the studs and hairclips necessary to hold everything together yet still keep our hair off our collars.

There wasn't even an apron to go with our new dresses. We had been advised that, when an apron proved necessary for the job we were doing, we would be provided with disposable ones.

I looked in the mirror with a wistful expression and reflected on what might have been. I felt like I had been lured there under false pretences and I don't think I ever quite got over the betrayal. I would follow third-year student nurses down the corridor and enviously covet their striped dresses and graceful apron ties. The third-year nurses got to keep their old uniforms as it must have been deemed cheaper to let them see out their training in their existing clothes rather than fork out for new ones that would only be needed for one year.

I consoled myself that I still got to pin on my traditional upside down, glow-in-the-dark nurses' watch, and my pen torch tucked into my top pocket nicely, next to all my different coloured ballpoint pens and my round-ended surgical scissors, so it wasn't all bad.

I enjoyed the work itself enormously but struggled with off-duty time. I've always found it difficult to integrate socially so living as well as working in a new environment proved to be quite a challenge for me.

When I came off duty at 4:15pm I would lie down on my bed and go to sleep. Partly because I needed it—we were worked extremely hard as student nurses and Baby Ben had dragged me out of bed at an unearthly hour to get me on the ward most days for 7:45am—but partly because I just needed to switch off. Most of the other girls would come off the ward and make plans for an evening out in the city or a get-together amongst themselves but I always found it hard to participate in out-of-hours activities.

My upbringing contributed largely to this mindset. I grew up in a very strict environment, and I was told that Christian girls did not go out into town nor, indeed, do most things that other people did. I had never been allowed to develop friendships with anyone because my mother inevitably would disapprove and not let me go to any events that were happening.

I suppose, for some people, that would mean that when they, at last, got out from the influence of a controlling parent, they would go mad doing all the things they had never been allowed to do, but it had the opposite effect on me. My mother seemed to have some sort of restrictive, sub-conscious hold over me all my life.

Working with the patients was great, though. I had a purpose in life. I was there to nurse all these sick and convalescing people and help make them better.

The regime at that time in NHS hospitals was very strict.

Matron was still the terrifying, exacting figurehead Who Must Be Obeyed. She had the last say about everything. Even the consultants were in awe of her.

Under her were the Number Sevens. Why they were so called, I have no idea. They were sort of unit managers and were in charge of the various departments of the inpatient section of the hospital.

Then there were the Ward Sisters. They varied in their approach to nurses and patients, but they could make your life totally miserable if they chose to.

Under the Sisters were the Staff Nurses, although some wards also had a Deputy Sister.

Staff Nurses were fully qualified, State Registered Nurses (SRNs), and had a couple of years' experience under their belts. Literally. They wore belts once they were trained.

We still had State Enrolled Nurses then (SENs), whose training had been tailored more to practical, rather than academic, methods of learning, so subsequently they were not given quite so much responsibility and their pay grade was lower.

Then came 3rd-Year Student Nurses, 2nd-Year Student Nurses, and then, the lowest of the low, 1st-Year Student Nurses.

The year you were in was vitally important, and we had fabric stripes that we had to sew onto our uniform sleeves to denote how far we had clawed our way up the ladder, so other medical professionals would know whether to defer to us, speak to us, or simply climb over us, depending on where we were in the pecking order.

There were also Auxiliary Nurses, who, although they had probably been on the same ward since before the electricity had been installed, and had gained more experience than the rest of the qualified staff had ever known, they were only ever allowed to make beds, help with meals, and bathe the patients.

There was a maid to every ward, and woe betide anyone who stepped on her newly washed floor area of the ward. The windowsills, bed frames, over-the-bed light fittings, curtain rails, lockers, and tables were damp-dusted every day and if a fragment of dust was ever found anywhere on the ward, somebody's job would be on the line. Not a germ could survive on the disinfected ward floors of MRI in those days.

We learnt so much during our training, and we were taught in such a way that we did not forget it. We were kept away from the general public for the first twelve weeks in the School of Nursing, although we still had to wear our uniforms every day, and they had to be worn properly. There was a teaching room next to the classroom, and we learnt how to make beds and bandage each other.

Sister Tutor would pair us off and stand over us whilst we put the bottom sheet on. With one student on each side of the bed, we would prise open the stiffly folded, starched sheet and spread it out.

'Do not waft it around, girls!' she would shout over all the giggling that went on.

'You have a sick patient in this bed, and they do not want to be surrounded by draughts!'

Tuck the top end in first. Hold up the side portion at an angle, fold the corner inwards, then tuck the side under the mattress. Tuck the bottom end in, hold up the side portion, fold the corner inwards, tuck in the side to create perfect envelope corners, and make sure everything is tight and nothing is sticking out.

Repeat. And repeat. And repeat. For twelve weeks.

We progressed to tucking in draw sheets and then the top sheets and counterpane as time went on.

We learnt how to change the bed with the patient still in it, without any dirty linen touching any clean linen, and if any bedding touched the floor at any stage, we had to start the whole process again.

1. Roll the patient to one side.
2. Loosen the bottom sheet, draw sheet and plastic sheet, roll up together towards patient.
3. Roll up clean bottom sheet lengthwise, leaving half on mattress. Tuck in top end, hold side portion, fold corner (as above), place rest of rolled sheet *near* dirty rolled sheet but without touching.
4. Repeat with draw sheet and plastic sheet.
5. Roll patient on to other side. (Sore, sick patient has to roll over four rolled-up lumps of laundry).
6. Remove dirty sheet by rolling towards the nurse. Place immediately in dirty laundry trolley.
7. Roll nice clean sheet towards nurse, tuck top end in, hold side portion, fold corner, etc.

It worked, but I suspect the patient benefitting from our tender ministrations would be feeling decidedly seasick by the time we'd finished. It was good being the dummy patient in the teaching room, though. You got a lie down for a while.

We also learnt how to clean a bed after a patient had been discharged, ready for the next one.

1. Strip the bed of all dirty linen, placing immediately into dirty laundry trolley. Hold it at arm's length, do not let it touch your uniform.
2. Make up a disinfectant solution in a bowl using hot water and Lysol.
3. Using a paper towel, wash entire mattress and plastic-covered pillows, ensuring no areas are missed.
4. Turn mattress over and wash underneath.
5. Using a fresh paper towel, wash the metal bed head and foot bars of the bed frame.
6. Using a fresh paper towel, wash each leg of the frame, paying particular attention to the wheels.
7. Using a fresh paper towel, wash the inside and outside of bedside locker and dry thoroughly.
8. Using a fresh paper towel, wash the surface of the bed table, then the legs.

All the cleaning procedures were carried out with us nurses clad in disposable plastic aprons, and we had to wash our hands constantly. Gloves were only used for dressing changes, wound swabs, and particularly unsavoury dealings that involved solid bodily emissions. By the end of the first week just in training, our hands were red raw from washing and remained that way for the length of time that nursing was our vocation.

We spent many a hysterical hour injecting oranges with hypodermic needles and learning the difference between subcutaneous (under the skin) and intramuscular (into the muscle) injections, and ascertaining how not to paralyse your patient by administering the latter into a nerve instead of the muscle. It was just unfortunate that, when I was eventually let loose on a member of the tax-paying public, I was required to administer an intramuscular injection to a frail old lady. I sized up the area on her thigh and estimated the exact appropriate point by measuring with my fingers as we had been taught, got the nod of approval from my supervisor, aimed with my needle, as we had been taught, and *crunch*. This poor lady had not got a sliver of muscle on her leg and I hit the bone with my perfectly executed injection. I was so upset in case I had hurt the patient. Thankfully for her, she was not quite compos mentis and did not appear to have noticed, but I was very wary for a long time after when I gave IM injections. Every subsequent patient got prodded and assessed to make sure their fat content was sufficient enough to withstand my ministrations.

Back in the teaching room, our bandaged limbs were not deemed acceptable unless there was a flawless line of V shapes running *exactly* along the length of the area, facing the right direction and starting and ending precisely where instructed. No matter that the patient had only an inch of damage to his person: the bandage had to be applied according to the rules.

'We do not want to cut off anyone's circulation by a badly positioned bandage, do we, girls?'

Learning to create slings had us all in hysterics and had excellent potential for cutting off circulation. By any given lunchtime, we were all trussed up like chickens and the ones to extricate themselves quickest were the first in line in the dining room.

We had to have in-depth knowledge in other areas of practical application and some lessons were not quite so attractive as others.

We grew extremely familiar with urine samples. They came in all colours, amounts, fragrances, and receptacles when we were doing the job for real and not just playing at it when we were in school.

But in the teaching room, they came in jugs. Vast amounts of jugs.

We were instructed to pour a measure of urine out into a test tube, hold it up against the light to look at the opacity or cloudiness, we had to wiggle it around, smell it to check for offensive odour and check for obvious foreign bodies, blood, or calculi. We then had to dip test strips in, up to a specific level, to perform a urinalysis. The commercially produced strips had coloured squares on them which, once dipped, were then compared with the colours printed on the glass container. These types of test strips are still in use today, and they check for the presence of protein, glucose, nitrates, blood, and acidity. We also had to perform a specific gravity test to determine the density of the urine by dropping a little bob weight into the measured test tube of urine and seeing where it landed according to the scale marked on the glass, a test which can indicate a variety of clinical conditions but is not done routinely nowadays.

We all learnt to take the urine tests in our stride, and they became commonplace to us. What we tried to avoid at all costs were the stool samples. It wasn't deemed necessary to wear gloves to test urine, but we were allowed to use gloves for poking around in the stainless steel bedpans containing solid matter that were conveyed from patient to sluice room at arm's length. We were frequently required to check for foreign bodies, record the colour, texture, and smell, assess the amount and remove portions to be placed in sterile containers and sent off to the pathology laboratory for proper testing. If we were ever seen transporting an uncovered bedpan, we were severely reprimanded, from the other side of the ward at blaring volume, if necessary. It was commonplace for those in authority to tear us off a strip in front of the whole ward full of patients and the rest of the staff. After all, we were only student nurses. We didn't have feelings.

Most wards still had the old-fashioned stainless steel bedpans, plus glass urinal bottles on the men's wards. There were white paper bedpan covers and white paper bottle covers, both shaped and specially made for the job, hung up on strings in the sluice room. There was a gigantic, stainless steel machine with a huge, gaping opening into which you inserted the bedpan after measuring and emptying the contents and this noisy contraption would wash and sterilise a pan in seconds and had an adapted area for the bottles. When washed, everything would be hung up on racks to be kept warm until they were needed again. If there was a particular rush for bedpans, and they were needed again in a hurry, we had to be really careful that the pans had cooled down sufficiently from the scalding cleaning process before they were thrust under the next invalid bottom because they really could have caused skin burns.

The men's ward had different problems to contend with if a gentlemen was given a glass urinal bottle that was on the warm side. The nurse was required to wait a little longer to retrieve the used bottle if the warmth had caused expansion issues that needed time to revert back to normal. Appendages had been known to get stuck, but maybe that was just a boast from the male patients.

We were required to learn about every single drug that the patients were taking and if anyone was newly admitted who was on an unusual drug, we had to use our off-duty time to swat up from the current MIMS (Monthly Index of Medical Specialities) publication and find out what it was for and what the correct dosage should be. When we did the drugs round the following day, the staff member supervising us would quiz us on all the medication on the trolley and check whether we knew what we were dispensing and whether the dosage prescribed was safe. We also had to know about all the possible side effects for all the medication being taken, so if a patient was inexplicably taken ill, or more ill than they usually were, we had a starting point for treatment and could act swiftly.

We were taught about aseptic techniques, which were used when wounds were swabbed and redressed. We wore gloves and used dressings forceps. We had a clean hand and a dirty hand. You did not dip a cotton wool ball into the cleaning solution with the same pair of tweezers that had held a swab that had just touched the wound. It was an intricately choreographed procedure, which involved a lot of swapping of hands and if the wound covered a large area on the body, the patient was taken into the Treatment Room on the ward, which was used like a mini operating theatre to further prevent any chance of infection. Each pack we used was completely sterile and had been delivered, sealed, to the ward from the Central Sterile Services Department, which, as the name suggests was a whole department of the hospital.

Everything was industrially washed and autoclaved after use throughout the hospital, and we never heard of hospital-transmitted infections. Just about everything was made of stainless steel and used over and over again after being scrupulously sterilised. If a patient acquired an infection after an operation, it was quite a scandal and internal enquiries would hold investigations to get to the bottom of the cause.

The fight against germs in our hospital was real but the scrupulous attention to detail and our in-depth knowledge about cross-infection overcame most of the problems. A huge contributing factor as to why things were kept clean was because we constantly washed our hands and never, ever allowed any bedding or equipment to touch the floor.

All our uniforms were laundered within the hospital laundry, and we were expressly forbidden to wear our uniforms outside the hospital grounds. Nurses or visitors to the ward were never allowed to sit on the bed. The ward sister would never have any qualms about barking at a recalcitrant relative who was in breach of her ward hygiene regime. They really did rule the roost in every way, but in those days, it was expected and accepted.

All patients had to be in their beds, in their pyjamas or nighties, no wearing of tee shirts and jogging bottoms as happens nowadays, for the Consultant's Ward Round. They had to have washed faces, combed hair, and precisely made bedding with exactly the correct amount of sheet folded over the counterpane. The pillowcases all had to be straightened, with the opening facing away from the ward main door. The patients had to sit up straight, no matter that they were in there because they were ill, and pay attention to the doctor and his/her team who approached the bed.

No magazines were to be visible, bedside lockers were tidied, ashtrays emptied (!), and apple cores disposed of. If any patient made an attempt to nip off to the loo when the Consultant's arrival was imminent, a junior student nurse would be sent to haul them back, mid-flow if necessary.

The same junior nurse was also expected to know every medical detail about the patient, so as to intelligently answer the questions fired at them by the consultant. It reflected badly on the ward sister if her nurses did not know what was going on and if she was shown up, it did not bode well for the offending student over the next few shifts. Every pus-filled abscess dressing, infected sputum sample collection, and manual evacuation of constipated patients would mysteriously appear on that nurse's to-do list.

It certainly was in our own interests to keep our wits about us.

Folk were kept in hospital for a long time in those days—a week for an appendectomy, two or three weeks for a hysterectomy, and the prospect of a stay which lasted months if you were on the orthopaedic ward.

I remember one young woman who was having treatment and correction of her spine, and she was in a plaster bed. They had taken full body plaster casts and the poor lady had to lie completely on this plaster of Paris cast. It was like a white, body-shaped coffin, which had been split down its length so it was in two halves, reinforced with wooden framing and was lined with sheepskin so whichever side of her was up wasn't encased, just covered with bedding. Every two hours, the second side of the cast was placed on top of her so she looked like a plaster mummy, four strong bodies were commandeered, and she was turned over bodily, and the top part, which had been the bottom part, was then removed and the bedding put back over her. We would then give her a jolly good massage, and she didn't get one bedsore or pressure point because of our nursing attention. Two hours later, the process was reversed: she was like a spit roast. The whole contraption stood a little way above a wooden bed base, so if she was lying on her front, we would put books and a mirror below her, so she could read and see us, and if she was on her back, we could slide bedpans underneath the appropriately cut-out holes in the plaster form.

It was so undignified for her and I have no idea whether it achieved the desired correction or how long she was in it for altogether, but she bore it all with good grace.

CHAPTER 9

Where Do I Go To From Here?

I left nursing and moved on

Of course, we were equally well taught in the theory as well as the practical. Everything we learnt about human biology, physiology, and anatomy was in great depth, and we had regular exams to test our newly acquired knowledge.

It was like working full-time and, at the same time, having to sit A-Level exams every few months. The NHS certainly got their pound of flesh from student nurses with the training methods at that time.

We would spend eight or ten weeks on a ward, then two weeks in school, studying theory and taking exams, on a rotation that repeated over the three-year course. When we were on the wards, we had to complete practical assessments, and we were supervised by the ward sister who would sign off our most recent achievement in our progress report book. There would also be comments inserted by senior staff members, a bit like regular school reports. If we did not pass one stage, we were not allowed to progress to the next.

If we were on night shifts, we would be on with one other nurse, possibly a third-year student, and, although we knew who to bleep if there was an emergency, we were entirely responsible for that ward of about twenty-six ill or post-op patients. It was not surprising that our backs suffered. There was never enough manpower available to lift or turn patients properly and safely. If someone died, as folk were inclined to do around 5:00 am (not all of them, you understand, just the ones who were really ill), the rest of the ward just had to manage whilst we sorted out the deceased behind the curtains.

It was a very impressive, thorough training, second to none, but I was not so impressed with the Victorian, antiquated accommodation in the Nurses' Home, even when we were promoted from the first Nurses' Home and were moved into a different building, which was supposed to be an upgrade.

My room was certainly bigger and more comfortable but the facilities were much the same. Being such old buildings meant that they came with their own particular problems.

I remember being on night shift and asleep in bed during the day on one occasion, when I was aroused, very unceremoniously, and not by Baby Ben.

There were two guys standing at my door, dressed in overalls and protective hoods and face masks. I thought nuclear war had been declared whilst I had been asleep and no one had thought to tell me. Apparently, the nurses' home had a cockroach problem and these gentlemen had kindly come to relieve me of my share of the little creatures by fumigating my room, which necessitated me being turfed out of the way, so the bug infestation team could do their stuff and spray their noxious liquids.

Not to be done out of my sleep ration, I took some bedding (well shaken, in light of my recently acquired information), donned my dressing gown, located and climbed up the stairwell which led to the flat roof, and made my bed up there in the open air.

We were having a bit of a heatwave at the time and I promptly fell asleep in the hot sunshine. When I woke a few hours later, I returned to my still-gaseous room (but this was the 1970s, so a few stray fumes weren't considered a problem), and checked for the presence of fumigators or fumigatees. The room appeared to be empty of either, so I had another snooze until Baby Ben woke me up for the next night shift.

When I went on duty that evening, no night lights were needed on the ward once the main lights were turned off. My face was red hot and, with the combination of sun exposure and, no doubt, nuclear-related, toxic gases that I had inhaled that afternoon, I glowed like a firefly in the dark. Meanwhile, over the next few days, whilst my sunburn gradually receded, I spent my off-duty time brushing up myriad little corpses which had, in their pre-deceased state, crawled out of all the crevices in my living space, wanting to take their last gasp of air in company, rather than die alone behind a skirting board.

During my time at Manchester Royal Infirmary, I gained so much knowledge and experience in many areas of nursing care.

I did rotations on Orthopaedics, Male & Female Medical Wards, Surgical, Children's Ward over at St Mary's across the road, Obstetrics & Gynaecology, again at St Mary's, and—my absolute favourite—Theatre duty.

I loved the Operating Theatre. It was a little world of its own and had various ante rooms within the unit. There were piles of scrub uniforms to be changed into, as ward uniforms were not allowed in any part of the theatre, and rows of white clogs all lined up in the locker room. The clogs had antistatic soles and were required to be worn. Clearly the transmission of foot-related infections was not considered to be of any significance, as we all shared the same clogs!

I would hold the hand of nervous pre-op patients as they counted down from 10 as the anaesthetic took effect, and dodge the post-op patients' vomit as they surfaced from the anaesthetic gases that invariably made them sick.

I have held legs by the ankle whilst the surgeon revved up his Black & Decker and sawed them off at his end. That was quite commonplace if people with diabetes developed circulation problems and suffered from gangrene. Amputations were performed far more routinely then, more so than nowadays, when there is more emphasis on diabetic care and prevention. People generally prefer their limbs to remain attached, given the choice.

I have watched varicose veins being ripped out, abscesses drained—and measured the amount of pus that was extricated— and witnessed many appendectomies that were routinely performed in about ten minutes.

I frequently witnessed open-heart surgeries where the patients were put on the by-pass machines, which warmed and filtered the entire circulation of blood, so the heart could be stopped and made still, ready for the intricate procedure ahead. The technicians in charge of these machines were so casual and matter-of-fact about it all. You wouldn't think they were keeping somebody alive.

We had to scrub up and gown up in the room next to the main theatre and prepare the vast and complicated trolleys and stainless steel trays required for each procedure. There were lists that informed us of the tray content requirements of surgical instruments for specific operations and everything had to be retrieved from the massive autoclave, after being washed and sterilised, and laid out in the order they would be needed by the surgeon.

We would then take all this equipment, together with swabs, dressings, suture needles, and surgical thread into the main theatre and position everything in exactly the right place.

All the packs of swabs and dressings were sealed in such a way so the edges could be carefully separated by our gloved hands, and then the inner wrapped contents were dropped onto the sterile surface. They were then suitable to be touched by the sterile, gloved hands of the nurse who was actually assisting the surgeon, and she would lay these items on a tray within the working area.

Before any action could take place, though, and before the revered surgeon entered the room with his hands clutched together, every single swab and instrument had to be counted and the amount of each was marked down on a white board fixed to the wall. Consequently, each kidney dish containing bloodied or pus-covered swabs that were subsequently passed back to us student nurses during the operation had to be carefully inspected, separated out, counted, then marked off the board before being bagged up.

Basically, what went in had to come out. The patient was not sewn up until each swab and instrument count tallied on the board to ensure nothing had been left inside the person on the table. If the count did not tally, all the waste bags had to be searched and re-counted and always resulted in an irate surgeon demanding to know why he was required to work with idiots.

We assistant nurses soon learnt to pay attention in the first place.

I soon moved up to Clean Nurse status and really enjoyed assisting the surgeons directly. I would earn brownie points in my head if I correctly anticipated the surgeon's growling demand for the next instrument and already had it in my hand, ready to slap it into his, right way round, so it was ready to use. When the suturing was being performed, we got to cut the stitches at precisely the right length demanded by that particular surgeon. There was always a lot of tutting from behind the Big Man's mask if we were a fraction of an inch either way from where he would have liked it. The Theatre Sister was very encouraging, though, and always acknowledged us if we had done a good job.

The Gynae Theatre was not so satisfying though, when I was on my Obs & Gynae rotation. The majority of operations were either done on ladies of mature years who needed their pelvic contents hoisting back up to where nature had intended them to be and being secured there with surgical rope, or on those who needed everything taken away. Either way, the thought of it made you want to cross your legs and immediately do vigorous pelvic floor exercises.

There were also the procedures required as a result of sad and tragic losses where the mothers needed to have the remains of miscarriages that hadn't been passed naturally, removed and sometimes pregnancies were terminated.

There were very few terminations performed then, other than those which had been deemed necessary for medical reasons, and we were always given the option whether we wanted to be involved. I was very grateful that I was never involved in any form of termination, although I did go into the sluice room one day and saw a stainless steel kidney dish on the draining board of the sink, with a tiny, tiny, impeccably formed foot just protruding from under the cover. The foetus was about 26 weeks, perfect in every way but had been aborted, put into a dish, covered with a paper towel and left by the sink. It is unthinkable now for that to happen, but as recently as the mid-1970s, that was the way it was. It didn't stop it from being heart breaking though.

The Obstetrics rotation was delightful. I helped on the Antenatal Clinic and was allowed to prod and feel all the lumps and bumps of the growing babies and work out which way up they were and the difference between a head and a bottom when palpating. I listened in with the trumpet stethoscope and determined the stage of the pregnancy by the fundal height. There were very few pregnancy scans and the scans that were necessary were only done on mothers who were thought to have problems, so all predictions and prognoses were done by feel and instinct.

I saw many babies born, cut many cords, and weighed the infants. They all had to be labelled and recorded before being passed to their mothers. Dads were not usually allowed anywhere near a delivery room, and they were only just about tolerated on the ward during the couple of visiting hours in an afternoon. Mums were the priority, and they were kept in bed for the first couple of days, and we would bring the babies to them. There was still a nursery where the babies were kept, and they would be taken to their mums for breastfeeding but, more often than not, we would then whisk them away for nappy changing. Those that were bottle fed were kept in the nursery during the night so mums could get their sleep, and we got to feed them and change them and cuddle them. All the nappies were of the towelling sort and were provided and laundered by the hospital, along with the sanitary requirements for the mums. The emphasis was on allowing the mums to rest as much as possible before they went home, so we nurses got to be nursemaids as well.

When I returned from the statutory two-week summer break to start my third year of training in 1976, I had been allocated to a ward with a ward sister who developed a personal vendetta against me. She was perfectly okay with me initially, but she suddenly changed her attitude towards me and consistently put me on split shifts and then more night duty. I had already had a long run of night duty before the summer holiday, so I really needed to catch up on my training assessments, such as Total Patient Care, which could only be done during the day when the patients were awake and responding. That was also the summer when I had got married and her obsession with putting me on split shifts which meant extended late shifts, followed by next day early morning shifts, meant I couldn't get home very often.

I even appealed to the Senior Nursing Officer who was the sister's supervisor, but my shifts remained as they were, even though they were obstructing my training. I eventually found out the reason for her resentful attitude towards me.

Apparently, one of the other student nurses in my intake had recently run off with the ward sister's live-in boyfriend. This certainly explained her bad temper, but soon after this happened, I had been seen by the ward sister when I was walking back to the nurses' home one day with my fellow student who, unbeknown to me at that point, was the culprit who had upset the sister's domestic arrangements.

Sister obviously decided I was in on the Operation Pinch Boyfriend plot and proceeded to make my life very miserable.

I had already applied for a transfer to finish my training at Preston Royal Infirmary, because of getting married, by that stage, but I could not persuade the Matron at Preston to take me on. They seemed to be unwilling to encourage a transfer mid-course, so by that Christmas, it had all become too stressful to continue at Manchester so, very reluctantly, I gave in my notice and returned home to live.

CHAPTER 10

I Know I Need To Be In Love

The day we got married

Soon after we had got engaged in 1974, I had asked a lady from church to make my wedding dress for me. She was a friend of the family and I knew she could do marvellous things with her sewing machine. I had designed the dress myself, so I explained what I wanted and what sort of fabric would work best and sent her on a mission to produce my dream wedding dress for the minimum amount of money. She did far better than I could have hoped, as she knew all the Preston market stalls that sold fabric, and she managed to get hold of a full bolt of fire-damaged satin off one of the traders, plus whatever else she needed, at a very good price.

The fabric on the inside of the bolt of satin was perfectly okay and without any marks or smoky smell, so she went ahead and made my dress. The finished garment cost me £15 and lay on the spare bed in my bedroom at my parents' house, covered over with a sheet, for nearly two years until our wedding day in 1976. I also paid many visits to Coupe's, the big haberdashery shop in Preston, to get all the bits necessary to make a veil and headdress.

I struggled to get appropriate shoes, as I couldn't afford the typical, satin bride's shoes because I knew I could only wear those for one day and, in my mind, that would be a waste of money. I eventually found some cream and grey shoes which fit nicely, so I spent the next few weeks coating these shoes with layer upon layer of pump whitener that we used to use on our school plimsolls. I would let one layer dry for a week, then apply another one, and carry on doing that until, at a reasonable distance, my wedding shoes appeared to be white. I figured that if anybody wanted to crawl around, inspecting my shoes any closer, they were welcome to do so.

Eventually, the white coating wore off and I kept those shoes for many years after we were married and wore them regularly, so my frugality paid off.

There were so many things, in those days, that had to be done exactly right, for tradition's sake, so it was harder than you might think to go against the grain and improvise. Neither were there the resources that are so easy to access now. There were no computers, so no internet. Everything had to be located locally via the Yellow Pages telephone directory, which was delivered to each house on an annual basis.

The rest of the arrangements were... challenging, shall we say, as we had no money and my mother was reluctant to part with any of hers. It was all done very begrudgingly and could hardly be described as being a magical, special time. Thankfully, we could spread all the cost out over the two years of our engagement, but, because all my wages were being saved up for a deposit on our first house, there was nothing to spare.

It was very rare to rent property to live in, unless you were a student, and we hunted high and low for a decent house in a reasonable area. We eventually found one that was in the price bracket that we could get a mortgage for, but we soon realised why it was reasonably priced.

It wasn't fit to live in.

The window frames were rotten, with huge gaps where the glass failed to meet the frame. The wiring in the house was the original and was positively dangerous. The plumbing all needed replacing, there was no form of heating other than one open fireplace and the whole of the interior wall and ceiling surfaces were thickly coated in dirty, yellow, nicotine residue, caused by the previous resident who had, presumably, smoked themselves to death.

It was a daunting prospect, but we knew we couldn't afford anything better, so we put in an offer and procured our first house in Fulwood for £7,750.00. We had painstakingly saved up the £775.00 needed for the 10% deposit, by never going anywhere that cost anything to get in. Our leisure time had to cost us nothing, otherwise we didn't do it. Our free time activities were mainly church based, so they didn't cost us anything financially, and we never went in a café or coffee shop. If we went out for the day, I would pack up sandwiches, and we would take a hot drink in a tartan patterned flask that incorporated two plastic cups, one with a handle. I sometimes borrowed my dad's posh flask that had a separate compartment in the bottom which held a specially shaped milk bottle, so we could add the milk to our drinks as they were poured out. Generally, adding the milk to those sorts of flasks when the drink was prepared made everything taste peculiar, but we learnt to get used to the flavour.

Philip had done a third year at college, and then got a job at the local hospital, working as a Medical Laboratory Scientist in the Pathology Lab. Although it was an interesting job, it didn't pay very well, and he had only been there a year when we got married. He had to learn plumbing and wiring skills very rapidly at the School of Trial and Error, because the only jobs that were going to get done on our house were those we could do ourselves. Our labour came free, and we had plenty of enthusiasm and motivation at that stage, even if we lacked the expertise. To be fair, though, we did learn quickly and everything got done properly.

My dad had taught me interior decorating, and I was an expert with a pasting brush and a roll of wallpaper. I always loved wall-papering rooms, so when Philip had finished writhing up the floor boards and hacking out channels in the plaster for wires and pipes, I was able to improve our living space by painting and papering. It was very slow progress, though, partly because we could only afford to buy materials a bit at a time, but also because the nicotine stains that covered every fixed surface in the house kept leaking through whatever I put on the walls. We had to strip off layers and layers of old wallpaper, some of which was woodchip, a popular type of wall covering at the time because it could be painted over and had a textured finish. It was almost impossible to remove, though, and we spent many hours, in the weeks running up to our wedding, covered in old paint flakes and old paste remnants, trying to hack off the old coatings, so we could put fresh paint and paper on. I ended up having to paint the walls with gloss paint to seal in the nicotine stains, and then I could emulsion the walls in the usual way. It took forever.

We did eventually decorate throughout, but we had to do it one room at a time and when we moved out , four and a half years later, we had just completed the final room only six weeks before.

Our wedding day had finally arrived. All the arrangements had been made. Dresses had been made for my two bridesmaids and suits had been bought for all the men and boys. The colour scheme was lilac for the bridesmaids and the flowers and Philip wore a wide lapelled, three-piece suit made from a blue, subtly checked fabric, with flared trousers. It was the height of fashion in 1976 and was teamed with a subtly patterned, pale blue shirt.

My dad had booked two weddings cars from a local firm that were supposed to be at our house in Penwortham well before 10:30

am, to get us to the church in the middle of Preston in time for the 11:00 am service.

I was all dressed and ready, apart from having forgotten to clean my teeth, so I was trying to squeeze my voluminous dress, complete with six-foot train into the very small bathroom, whilst navigating around the plentiful veil that was hampering the access to my teeth. My main problem was trying not to spit down my front and have toothpaste stains on my chest all day, while my dad was going ballistic down the phone to the wedding car company.

My dad was a very mild tempered man usually, but he was absolutely livid that the cars he had booked were, seemingly, wandering around Penwortham, hoping to find a woman in a white dress, presumably, thumbing a lift. I have no idea what address they had been given by their office, or why they were having trouble finding us, but my dad eventually got fed up of waiting, got in his own car and went out to look for them. There was no other way of contacting the drivers because there were no mobile phones in those days, so, unless they had stopped at a phone box and called back to the office, we were no nearer to finding them.

Meanwhile, the neighbour across the road had picked up on the situation and was now out with his duster, polishing his already sparkling, much cossetted, white Rover car, desperately hoping that he would be called upon to save the day and get me to the church on time.

Eventually, my dad returned to the house with the two errant shiny black cars, devoid of any occupants, in tow, the drivers of which he had instructed, in no uncertain terms, to follow him back to his house. They may have been somebody else's wedding cars for all we knew, but, possession is nine-tenths of the law. We needed cars. We had found cars. I think I am safe in the recollection that this car company had to deduct a hefty discount from their invoice before my dad parted with any money.

I arrived at the church half an hour late. All the specially chosen music had long since been played and the organist was on audience requests and suffering from repetitive strain injuries. The guests were all restless and muttering and most were firmly convinced that I'd changed my mind and I wasn't coming.

Instead of the leisurely gathering together of the bridal party on the church steps for photographs, it degenerated into a jumble of satin train, crumpled veil, and mixed up bouquets, whilst we tried to assemble ourselves in the correct order for the walk down the aisle.

The first distinctive notes of the Bridal March from Lohengrin were heard and I, at last headed down the aisle on my dad's arm. I was too flustered to be nervous, but I did detect a lot of notes from Jonathan, the organist, that shouldn't have been there, and some missing that should have been present. By the time I reached the front of the church, the music had all but fallen apart, as Jonathan's overworked fingers got themselves in a complete knot and stopped abruptly.

North Road Pentecostal Church did not have its own registrar, so an official from the Registry Office had to attend to the legal requirements at any wedding held there. This caused extra problems because the lady booked to officiate at our wedding ceremony at 11:00 am had other weddings to attend. This was August, after all, and the height of the wedding season.

There was a lot of furious whispering going on and then an announcement was made that the service would have to be done a different way round. I was so glad we had paid all that money for the printed Order of Service, only to have it all upended. So, instead of the vows, then the sermon, then the signing of the register in the vestry, we had to sign the register immediately after the vows, and then all traipse back into the church and have the sermon afterwards. This meant that the accommodating, patient registrar could still make it to her next booking if she left immediately, broke the speed limit, and missed her lunch.

In those days, tradition was followed to the letter, so all this re-arrangement was most inappropriate and very unsettling. Nevertheless, the immediate family all sat back down and obediently listened to the sermon and sang the final hymn. Then came the organisation of the wedding party to get us all back down the aisle with the correct partners. It was all done in a very undignified manner and involved a lot of shuffling around people in the confined space in the front pews of the church.

Jonathan was in good form and had decided, without checking whether we were all actually ready to leave, that enough was enough. He was ready for his lunch and this service had gone on too long for his liking already. He struck up the opening chords of Mendelssohn's Wedding March (well, approximately), and set off at a galloping pace. Philip and I had paired off and that was all that mattered, so we set off at a sprint back down the other aisle to exit the church, leaving everyone else to sort themselves out and follow on when they had found someone to link arms with.

We arrived outside on the church steps a little out of breath, but we were all able to position ourselves properly and smile serenely for the photographer, who, incidentally, wasn't the man we had booked, but his assistant, who wasn't anywhere near as professional as he should have been. This second reserve man had clearly not paid attention on the training day, which taught them how to position a bride's train to show it off properly in the photographs, nor had he remembered to bring the pre-requested guest book to the church and reception for people to sign.

Once the requisite church photos had been captured, we all piled into the official cars and departed, in a cloud of confetti, to Barton Village Hall.

The 7th of August 1976 was one of the hottest days, in the hottest summer on record. All the men were suitably kitted out in their three-piece wool blend suits, stiff, fastened shirt collars with ties and fast melting Brylcreem-ed hair. Most of the female guests had dresses or skirts with matching jackets or coats and it just was not the done thing to divest oneself of any items of the carefully put together wedding outfit in order to perspire a little less. My dress was long sleeved with tight, many buttoned cuffs, high necked, high waisted, made from good quality, thick satin, overlaid with lace in parts, to which a heavy, long train was attached. An itchy headdress with voluminous veil completed my summer ensemble and I sweated along with everyone else. That was the fashion of the day, so we just put up with it.

The day was brilliantly sunny, which most brides long for, but we were all squinting at the photographer who had trailed us out onto the bowling green at Barton, with the ladies' high heeled shoes sinking into a meticulously preserved lawn, which we probably completely ruined for the rest of that season's bowling enthusiasts. The face-ache and spasmodic twitching set in early, compounded by the squinting and, by the time we were allowed to retreat to the relative cool of the village hall, we could barely focus our eyes or speak properly.

We were met with an enticing spread of ham salad (the photos of the reception were liberally dotted around with bottles of Heinz Salad Cream), with cream cakes to follow. The square, three tiered wedding cake with lacy royal icing took pride of place in the centre of the top table and I seem to remember we spent all of the reception trying to peer around this decorated masterpiece to see who was sitting at the other tables. The cake was, of course, fruit cake. No other options would have been deemed suitable or fitting, as small pieces of cake were traditionally given or posted out in tiny cake boxes after the event to people who had been invited to the wedding and were unable to attend. The cake had to be substantial enough to keep fresh and hold its shape as long as possible.

The smaller top tier was often kept from the wedding to use as a christening cake, because, only as recently as a decade earlier, contraception was not routinely practised, which meant that nature would probably take its course within the first year of marriage and so the cake would still be edible and welcome at the first baby's celebrations.

The reception couldn't have lasted very long because we were back in Woodplumpton by late afternoon. We had first called into Inskip Baptist Church graveyard as I wanted to put my bouquet on Philip's dad's grave. By then, of course, the geographically challenged wedding car drivers had already gone off to wander aimlessly around the other suburbs of Preston that they hadn't covered that morning, due to being interrupted by some woman wanting a lift to church, so I was squashed into our little Wolseley Hornet car, with my dress stuffed in wherever it would go. We arrived at Inskip, where, to my horror, we realised the annual church convention, which used to be held in a marquee in the grounds of the church, was in full flow and, because the weather was so hot, the marquee sides had all been rolled up to allow maximum air circulation.

There must have been a couple of hundred people who were all instantly distracted from the over-heated preacher's exhortations, and treated to the spectacle of me being extracted from a very small car with a very big dress that was, by now, a crumpled, slightly damp, heap of fabric. It was the most inelegant, embarrassing, emergence imaginable and was done with a full audience. I then had to pick my way, very precariously between the grave stones, trying not to catch my dress on anything and gather my train into some semblance of order, still clutching my bouquet, knowing that every step was being watched.

It was not the poignant and reflective moment either of us had envisaged, but we did what we had gone there to do and then repeated the whole spectacle in reverse as we made our way back to the car, stuffed everything back in and drove away, hoping that there weren't various leftover bits of me hanging out of the door frame.

When we got back to where Philip's mum lived, I changed into my going away outfit, which I was very proud of. It had been a good find several months earlier in the January sale. Consequently, this dress and jacket were made from a lovely wool fabric, fully lined and just the thing for the hottest summer on record. I had shoes and bag to match, but there was no time to stand and admire the finished effect.

Philip's brother had offered us his car to take on honeymoon because it was more reliable than ours, but he was absolutely paranoid that the guests—or more specifically, The Cousins—would find out and trim it up with shaving foam, ribbons, and tin cans, as was the custom. He had parked it round the back of the farmyard, out of sight, and wanted us to make a dash for it and drive it away before his prized possession was sabotaged and the paintwork ruined. That was easier said than done, but we managed to escape with the minimum of shaving foam and confetti showers and set off on our honeymoon.

It was early evening when we arrived in Cumbria and, after the manic rush and bustle of the day, the peace and quiet was such a contrast.

We had no money to spend on extras so when I had seen a Farmhouse Bed & Breakfast plus Evening Meal advertised in a local holiday brochure for a very reasonable price a few weeks earlier, I had booked it for our honeymoon.

It turned out that the advert had been a mistake and there was no evening meal included so we spent the week eating biscuits and crisps as we couldn't afford meals out. There were no cheap, fast food outlets in those days, not even pub food. With our strict upbringing, neither of us would have dared darken the doors of one of those public houses in any case. We would surely have been struck with a lightning bolt or worse!

The other, slightly disconcerting, revelation about our accommodation for the week was that our room had a glass door! It was literally a room in the family home, with all the facilities shared, so we addressed this somewhat awkward situation by hanging everything we could find on the door hook and spreading it out as wide as possible.

As we unpacked, we realised that neither of us had thought to pack a towel and there were none provided at the B&B. We knew there were about 105 brand new towels, bought for us as wedding presents, all nicely displayed on Philip's mum's dining table back home, along with the many other generous gifts we had received, so we were quite annoyed to have to go into a shop in the town and buy a towel, which remained hard and completely unabsorbent all week because we couldn't wash it to soften it up.

We would go out each day and find (free) places to explore, using the ordnance survey map we had brought with us. We would try and match the road signs with the map, but, every single day, we would find ourselves traversing one or other of a country road that got narrower and narrower, until grass started to appear down the middle, shortly before we were brought to an abrupt halt by a gate leading to a field. We reversed down most of the local roads that week.

I have to say, there have probably been more luxurious honeymoons on record.

We arrived back home at the end of the week and, after we had gone inside and looked around, there seemed to be something a little odd about the house, but we weren't sure what it was. Things were in strange places and some of the larger pieces of furniture had marks or scrapes on them. We were to find out later that The Cousins who had been foiled in their attempts to dress up the honeymoon car had got their revenge by 'gaining entry' (the less said about that, the better) to our house and transferring quite a few items that normally lived downstairs to the upstairs, including the only new kitchen item we possessed which was a shiny fridge/freezer. One of Philip's brothers, who had got wind of this, had recruited some muscle and gone in (with a key) and done his best to put everything back where it should be. The scars on the furniture remained to bear witness to the sneaky activity that had taken place whilst we were away.

CHAPTER 11

Bless The Beasts And The Children

*When we decided having pups and a
baby was a good idea*

After I had left nursing, I got a job working at Plumbs Stretch Covers in Preston. They were, and still are, a company that made fitted, stretch covers for chairs and sofas. I was in the office and was involved in the statistics for the factory items. When I first started there, the office was located in the far corner of the factory, which meant we had to walk past all the vast bolts of fabrics and the enormous cutting machines, and we could watch the covers being made from cutting to sewing. I found it fascinating. There were five of us in the office and it was a great place to work.

After a few months, the office was moved and relocated upstairs, to a corner of a huge, empty area of the factory. I have no idea why this happened, but it was a bizarre space to work in. It was there that I learnt to budget with the household expenses. We were paid in cash every week, and we would go down to the cash office, next to the clocking in machine at the entrance to the building, and be handed a square, brown envelope. We would all scurry back upstairs, make a cup of tea and count the contents meticulously, down to the last penny.

Then we made a list of all our outgoings—food, petrol, milkman, newspapers, etc.—and every week we would bemoan the fact that there was not enough left. Our manager never minded us doing all this personal housekeeping during work time: indeed, she was doing it herself over at her own desk.

Philip and I were quite forward thinking, and as soon as it was possible to have direct debits set up at the bank to pay all our larger, regular bills, we preferred to do that. Until then, though, we paid everything by cheque, but most bills used to come with a pre-paid envelope so it was straightforward enough to post our cheques off to the relevant companies.

I had been at Plumbs for about seven months when I started to feel a little unwell. I was a bit queasy now and again and, taking into account the fact that there had been other clues, we wondered if I was pregnant. You would think that this would be an easy theory to clarify but, in 1977, it wasn't.

There was no such thing as nipping to the chemist and buying a testing kit. Anything that could possibly be purchased was very expensive and unreliable. Philip was working at the Path Lab in the hospital, so we decided he would take advantage of his position and find someone who would perform a pregnancy test.

So, one morning, he went to work, clutching a bottle containing my sample, alongside his sandwiches and when he arrived, he found someone who was qualified in such things and left it with them to do the deed. I had the strange experience later that afternoon, even for those days, of my husband ringing me at work to tell me I was pregnant! Normally, the wife would have missed two or three periods, taken herself off to the GP, who would have sent a sample off to the hospital, and then she would have found out the result in due course. She would have told her husband, possibly over a romantic dinner. I got to find out about our firstborn in amongst stock lists of king size duvet covers and washable, stretch sofa covers.

I continued working until that Christmas. At that time, maternity benefit was paid for around eleven or twelve weeks before the birth and eight weeks after, plus we got a one-off maternity grant, which was a lump sum designed to cover the cost of a pram, cot, nappies, and basic requirements. There was also a tax rebate for the husband, back to the start of that tax year, so if you timed it right, as we did, you could get a whole year's tax back. I only got this package once, though, as I was not employed for any of my other pregnancies, and, as now, the rules changed every couple of years.

Plumbs did Christmas in style for their employees. We were all given bonus pay packets, chocolates, and wine, if you wanted it, and there had been an impressive Christmas dinner laid on in the canteen beforehand. The factory closed for the Christmas period and I started my maternity leave. I was very sad not to go back.

Fairly soon after we got married, we had bought a Golden Cocker Spaniel, which we named Mandy. I seem to recall we also got a credit card round about then, which explains how we could afford some of the purchases we made when we were newly married. When I was still living in the nurses' home, I used to arrive back home from Manchester on the bus for my two days' off duty and Philip would meet me at the bus stop with this tiny puppy tucked into his jacket.

Shortly after I started my maternity leave, we seemed to think, for some inexplicable reason, it was a good idea to get Mandy in pup. We did some research and found a reputable breeder who was fairly local and took her along for a bit of courting. Bobby, the sire dog, was a very handsome Blue Roan spaniel who had won awards at Crufts and had an excellent pedigree. We introduced the two animals and left them to get to know each other in a shed-type building, whilst we stood around, trying to look anywhere but where the action was, making awkward conversation with a guy whom we'd only just met, for the sole purpose of a somewhat delicate and personal activity. The deed was finally done, and we went back home with the instruction from Bobby's owner to go back and do it all again in two days' time, 'just to be sure'.

Sure enough, Mandy was confirmed as pregnant a few weeks later and was thought to be due towards the end of March. My baby was due 25th February, and in our naivety, we thought that by the time the pups came, we would be all organised, back to normal and have this parenting thing well and truly nailed.

My due date came and went and I attended the official opening of our church, Fulwood Free Methodist Church, complete with my considerable bump still intact. I had started to develop problems with my pregnancy, and I suspected, from my antenatal training in Manchester, that I had pre-eclamptic toxaemia. This is a very serious condition that, if left untreated, many pregnant women used to die from. It got worse over a few days, and I was retaining fluid and had all the symptoms of very high blood pressure. I went to bed as I was feeling very ill. We phoned the doctor, who didn't really believe me because I had been for all my antenatal care and everything had been fine up until that point. Nevertheless, she said she would come and see me at home that lunchtime.

It must have been a weekend because Philip was at home and had brought Mandy up to see me. Mandy liked her home comforts and enjoyed actually getting under the duvet and snuggling down, just out of arm's reach. Just as the dog had got nicely settled somewhere around my knees, which I hadn't seen or touched for some months, the doorbell rang and Philip shot downstairs to answer it, leaving me, who had the agility of a beached whale, to try and squirm about to locate the other lady-in-waiting in the bed, and evict her before the doctor appeared.

Our GP was a very strict old-school type doctor, and she was extremely intolerant of time wasters. If any patient wasn't properly ill when they went to see her, she had no compunction about telling them off about and instructing them to go back home. On the other hand, she was the most patient, reassuring, devoted, and knowledgeable lady, who would move heaven and earth to get you better when you were genuinely ill. She started to examine me and was only slightly distracted by me frantically signalling to Philip that the dog was still in the bed and needed removing before the examination got as far down as my hugely swollen ankles.

Thankfully, the doctor seemed to be oblivious to the surreptitious rummaging that was going on at the foot end of the bed, as Philip managed to reach under the duvet and extract a very warm dog and shoo her away down the stairs. The doctor would certainly have had something to say about the hygiene implications of sharing the bed with a dog.

She lost no time in prescribing me some very strong tranquilisers called Ativan. This drug was routinely prescribed for pre-eclampsia and other conditions that may have led to seizures. I have since looked up the contraindications and side effects in the modern packaging:

Warning, do not use Ativan if you are pregnant.

It can cause birth defects or life-threatening withdrawal symptoms in a newborn.

It then goes on to describe all manner of things that will happen if taken for a prolonged period, including addiction and death.

So, with complete and innocent faith in my GP, I took those tablets for two weeks pre-natal and six weeks post-natal, because I was told to.

When I was three weeks overdue, I was taken into hospital to be induced. Every day, I was told that today would be the day, and every day there would be some reason why I hadn't been induced. Philip would come upstairs to the ward from where he worked in the Path Lab and he would take my daily blood sample for testing, along with those from all the other pregnant ladies.

I was even taken to the X-ray department one day because one of the doctors was convinced I wasn't as overdue as my dates suggested, and ultrasound scans were not readily available then. I was asked to lie on the bed, where they fastened a strap around my abdomen, *extremely* tightly, to keep the baby still, they said, and then they took the first x-ray. Then I was told to turn over and lie on my tummy whilst the second x-ray was taken! Looking back, it just does not bear thinking about, but, that's the way it was, and they decided that the baby's bone density was compatible with the length of pregnancy, and so I was induced.

I was put on the Syntocinon drip that started strong contractions straight away. There was no gentle, gradual build, just full on labour pains, which went on for 10 hours. At some point, I was given Pethidine which did the strangest things to me and I felt completely out of control. It also made me violently sick, which I could well do without at that point; I felt I had enough to be going on with. Philip was allowed to be in the delivery room but only under great sufferance. The old-school midwife who was looking after me kept telling him off for looking at the monitors and the charts.

'You're not here to be looking at those things, Father!' she barked at him. 'Just you pay attention to your wife!'

I can't help thinking she should have hired herself out on a subscription package, so she could visit each postnatal home at monthly intervals, and bark the same instruction to every inattentive husband on a regular basis.

For a minimum of two years.

After each child.

David James finally made his appearance at 6:10 pm on the 22nd of March, but not without incident. As his head was born it was clear that the cord was wrapped firmly around his neck more than once and, thankfully, my very experienced, if a little tartly tongued, midwife dealt with the errant cord very efficiently by hacking it off in pieces as rapidly as she could, and releasing the rest of his body safely. Until writing this account, I'd never really realised just how hazardous David's pregnancy and birth had been, because we humans just tend to cope with whatever is challenging us at the present moment. It's only when we look back at the whole picture and think, Wow! God was really looking after us. So, David—well done, lad!

He was definitely very overdue—three and a half weeks late—and his skin was so dried up I had to rub tons of baby oil over it several times a day. The downside of all the traumatic happenings was that I had post-natal depression almost from day one. I realise now that the medication I was on would not have helped, and he was so drowsy and flat for days until the effects worked out of his system. The upside was that we both got plenty of sleep!

I was kept in hospital and not allowed out of bed until the symptoms of the pre-eclampsia had reduced sufficiently for the danger of seizures to abate but I had to take the tranquilisers for a long time afterwards. As a consequence, I found it difficult to bond properly with David. He was an absolutely model baby—woke up once in the night to feed and be changed then back down to sleep until a civilised time. By the time I was taken off the drugs, he had found his own routine, which was to be a very subdued and pliable infant. It sounds idyllic but I don't think it was healthy. I suspect, even though he was tiny, he picked up on my depressed state and reacted accordingly, much like the little ones we see in orphanages in film footage of other countries, where the children are not given enough attention or stimulation.

I loved him very much but didn't know how to express that as much as I wanted to. It was also a remnant of my upbringing. I had never, ever been told that I was loved, nor was it expressed. There were no hugs or displays of affection from my mother, not even positive words. My childhood was not a carefree, relaxed period of time. It was tense and I just knew that life was there to be got on with and, if I had a problem, I had to sort it out myself. Unfortunately, I carried that ethos with me through into adulthood and, because David was my first child, he was the prototype and bore the brunt of my maternal failings.

I really regret that David got a raw deal in his formative years, but I am forever thankful that when he became an adult and could fend for himself, God had given him the strength of character to be able to defy any relationship defects he had learnt from me and go on to develop healthy, positive connections with people. He is such an outgoing, caring, compassionate man and, in turn, he is teaching these positive values to his children.

God always had all my children in the palm of his hand, even before they were born, but He needed me as a channel to bring them into the world and care for their physical needs.

When my children reached adulthood, God took each one and put them through His Finishing School. He undid a lot of the emotional damage that could have stayed with them, taught them truths that they hadn't yet learnt about themselves and counteracted a lot of negativity that they grew up with. They are not perfect and each will still have their own hang ups, and they have all experienced major upheaval in their lives, which they have dealt with in a Godly way. Because none of them have had an easy ride, I do feel they all have developed special gifts for engaging with others, and they all demonstrate a positive attitude to life that they did not learn from me. I give God all the credit for the lives they lead now.

Because of my reluctance to part company with my baby, the

synchronisation with the dog's pregnancy had gone somewhat awry. David was born on the 22nd and Mandy's seven pups were born on the 24th. Fortunately, she just got on with things and managed herself, which was just as well because we were otherwise occupied. Philip had made her a large whelping box out of plywood, which I had painted with white gloss paint for easy cleaning and which had a drop-down door so Mandy could escape when it all got too much. So, for the next couple of months, it was very much a crèche in our house and there was an awful lot of crying, feeding, and pooping going on, from one source or another.

In due course, the pups were all found new homes by the wonderful and very effective medium of advertising in the local paper. Prospective owners came to coo over the gorgeous, velvety bundles and choose which one they would like to buy. We had different coloured puppy collars, so we could identify each pup. Of course, we knew exactly which was which, but we had to prove that to the person who had just parted with their deposit. Once a pup has a collar to confirm its reserved status, the breeder becomes slightly paranoid in case that particular pup is the very one which will fall ill or hurt itself, or die.

Although Mandy had produced the pups without any help, she wasn't a brilliant mother and got very fed up with them hassling her as they got bigger. I think she was quite glad when the last one left, and she could resume her rightful place on the sheepskin rug in front of the fireplace, undisturbed.

We took a holiday in September that year and, as always, we tried to make it happen as cheaply as possible. We borrowed a tent. Yes. A tent.

It was a six-berth frame tent that we had never seen erected, but how hard could it be? I had been camping many times, and we had, or could borrow, most of the other equipment we would need, so we would manage very nicely.

We had a five-month-old baby, carry cot, pram, towelling nappies, bucket to soak dirty nappies in, washing powder for when we found a launderette to wash towelling nappies in, lots of wooden clothes pegs and spare washing line to attach to tent to dry towelling nappies on, cooking equipment, baby equipment—you get the picture. And yet, we thought it was a good idea.

We even had another idea. Instead of staying relatively close to home in case of things not going as well as we would have liked, we booked a campsite in Cornwall. Land's End to be precise.

By this stage, Philip had left his job at the Path Lab and bought a milk round. He managed to conscript some stand-in staff to run his milk round whilst we were away, and he decided that he would do a double delivery on the Friday evening which would see his customers over the weekend. He had managed to get very little, if any, sleep that day, due to packing up the car, collecting his milk round money in the afternoon and delivering all evening.

He got home around midnight, we finished packing everything into our car, which proved to be nowhere near big enough, and we set off for an overnight journey. There was a slight hitch, even before we set off, in that David had developed a tummy bug, the consequence of which was diarrhoea and vomiting. Undeterred, we packed plenty of glucose water, which I had prepared earlier, and headed off into the night.

I think we must have stopped off at some motorway services and had a sleep in the car for a few hours because we were still on the motorway when the sun came up and, even in those days, it didn't normally take more than eight hours to get to Cornwall. The day was heating up early and, as we drove along, we remarked on how many cars we had seen parked on the hard shoulder with their bonnets up and engines steaming.

Unfortunately, it wasn't long before we joined them. It was a common problem with the cars of that era to overheat on long journeys, and we found ourselves just into Exeter with an engine billowing white clouds of steam, a fully loaded, weighed down vehicle and a sickly baby on board. Philip had to trek along the hard shoulder to the nearest emergency telephone and call for help. We had no AA or RAC cover so the call was sent to a local garage who said they would send out a recovery truck but it may be some time. We were rescued eventually and towed into a garage in Taunton. It took a couple of hours to replace the cracked radiator, by which time, the day was starting to cool down so there was little risk of it overheating again. It was a good job we had a credit card, otherwise we would have had to sell David to pay for the radiator, and we really didn't want to have to do that, after all the trouble I'd gone to, to produce him in the first place. Besides, the sour, eye-watering smell that was emanating from him would have meant we would have had to let him go at a discounted price because he was soiled goods.

We finally rolled into the campsite just as the daylight was fading, about twenty hours since we had left home and, after the boiling hot day we had travelled down in, it had now decided to rain.

We found what looked like a suitable plot and some of the other campers very kindly helped us to make sense of the unfamiliar tangle of canvas, pegs, and guy ropes and assemble our tent in the half-light, at least enough so it would stay up overnight and shelter us from the rain that was increasing in intensity. We located the essentials such as the beds, camping stove and kettle, heated some soup, and went to bed.

We woke up the following morning to another glorious day and went outside to have a proper look at where we had arrived and get an idea of what our surroundings were like. It took a remarkably short amount of time for us to look down and realise that we were not alone on our chosen plot of land. Just about everything around us appeared to be moving, and we were horrified to discover that we had pitched on an ant's nest and the little blighters were warming up nicely in the sun and investigating their new neighbours. All I can say is that the inside bedroom of our tent must have been extraordinarily sealed because there didn't appear to be any ants on the bedding at all, so that was a blessing.

Our trusty camping neighbours rallied round again, and the tent was frogmarched across the campsite, with a man on each corner pole and an assortment of trailing guy ropes, to a pitch area that I had personally inspected minutely and pronounced to be safe, with no sitting tenants.

The rest of the holiday was perfect. We had glorious sun for ten days, David recovered from his tummy issues quite quickly, we were near a beach, and it was in the days before Land's End had been commercialised, so it was a lovely area to explore—and cheap.

The day we packed up and took the tent down, the heavens opened and it poured down the ten days' worth of rain it had been saving up. We rolled the soggy tent up as best we could, which meant it took up twice as much room in the car as it should have done, stuffed everything in, and made our way back home. We had to put up with a steamy car on the return journey also, but this time the steam was inside the car, emanating from its wet contents that started to smell quite badly by the time we got home. This time, we couldn't blame David for the odour, but it took days to get the tent dried out in our garden, so it could be folded properly and put away in storage. Hot tip—never put a wet tent away until next season. You will live with the smell for your entire holiday and the black marks of mildew are not very attractive. Ask me how I know!

During the renovations of our house, we had installed a new gas fire. This fire turned out to be multifunctional. Not only did it provide warmth that winter, known as the Winter of Discontent, because of all the trade union members' strike actions in defiance of Prime Minister James Callaghan's attempts to control inflation, but it proved to be the sole method of cooking our meal on more than one occasion. It was a very cold winter and, due to frequent industrial unrest, there were intermittent power cuts throughout, so we used to toast bread and crumpets on the gas fire, using a long, brass, toasting fork. It was quite a skill, as the crumpets kept falling off the fork because of their holey texture, and invariably landed inside the metal guard on the front of the fire. There were some grease-based, burnt on marks that never did clean off that fire, but it was all in a good cause. Because the rest of the house was so cold, David was regularly bathed in the baby bath in front of the fire, which we had filled with jugs of hot water (I did cool it down and check the temperature before I put him in. I wasn't completely stupid), in amongst the towelling nappies which were hung over the maiden to dry. During the power cuts, the room was lit by candles, supplemented by the glow from the fire; all very cramped, but very cosy as long as we didn't move from the room.

I developed a habit which lasted for decades, of always having plenty of utility candles and matches in the house because, either due to industrial action by various union members over the years, or lightning storms striking vital power stations and causing blackouts, we had to keep our wits about us and be prepared for every eventuality.

CHAPTER 12

Ticket To Ride

The trauma of learning to drive

After the traumatic experience of my first pregnancy and birth, I was never, ever, having any more children.

Never.

Anybody who had gone through labour more than once needed their bumps felt, in my opinion, so, no. No more babies.

I have no idea, then, why I was being booked in at the antenatal clinic, in the early months of the following year. I think my drug-addled brain must have blanked out all my determined resolutions and there I was again, permanently nauseous and already gaining weight.

I also, for reasons unknown, thought it would be a good idea to start having driving lessons, whilst pregnant. I suppose it was a practical necessity but I failed to factor in the stress and anxiety having driving lessons and taking a driving test may engender.

I had previously had a few driving lessons on a fairly informal basis, but they had not had happy outcomes. A friend of my dad's had offered to take me out for lessons a few years earlier but as the guy was patiently explaining the mechanics of starting the engine and releasing the clutch and balancing the accelerator, all I could think of was, 'Never mind all that. Just show me where the brake is, that's the important pedal.' I wasn't bothered about moving forward, I just wanted to know how to stop the thing.

I drove a few times but I didn't make much progress because I had no confidence and, rather than keep putting the poor man through any more needless stress, as portrayed by his whitening knuckles as he grasped hold of the seat next to me, I politely declined any further offers by him to take me out in his car again.

Just after we were married, Philip decided it was high time I got myself mobile and manfully offered to teach me to drive. Mistake number one, you might think, but no, it actually went quite well. He was very patient and if we had both ended up in the canal, I don't think he would have reacted with anything stronger than 'Good Heavens!' The problem lay with the fact that we could only afford to run very old cars which kept going wrong and breaking down, so he wouldn't let me drive anything that was unreliable.

The crux of the matter came when I was driving to my parents' house one Saturday afternoon. The journey had gone well. I did not grind any gears, I had generally driven in a straight line, stopped at most of the red lights and even used the wing mirrors, which were actually located on the wings of cars at that time. I had successfully turned left off the main road and wound my way cautiously down the minor road which led to their road. I made a right turn onto their road and immediately attempted to turn left into their drive which ran along the side of the house. Unfortunately, that was the point at which the old banger we owned decide it had had enough of steering properly and promptly jammed itself in a left-sided trajectory, causing the nearside of the car to start travelling up the flower bed instead of the driveway. Whilst I was frantically trying to yank the steering wheel to the right to get out of the flower bed—mainly because I was imagining my mother's reaction—Philip was rapidly preparing to meet his Maker, as the front bedroom corner of the bungalow wall loomed towards him at a great rate of knots. He was almost at the point of making an exclamation, when I made the executive decision to practice my emergency stop. Thankfully, it was only the steering system which had failed, and the brakes still functioned normally and the car stopped moving.

We both sat there trembling for half a minute or so before I dared glance over at him. He had gone very grey-looking and again, there were white knuckles belonging to hands gripping the passenger seat next to me.

'What... were... you... doing?' he asked, very quietly. That was a bad sign. I was in trouble. I started to proclaim my innocence and that it wasn't me, it was the car, but he clearly was not convinced. It was only as he and my dad investigated the car after plenty of hot, sweet tea had been imbibed, and our facial colour had returned to normal, that it was proved to be, indeed, the car's fault. Even so, he never let me drive again after that episode.

Bit of an over-reaction, really. After all, I didn't actually hit anything. There was a good inch between my mother's front bedroom window and the front bumper of the car.

It was decreed, therefore, that this next attempt at making me legal behind the wheel of a car would be done properly. Philip's uncle was a professional driving instructor and did not stand any messing, so if I did not learn by any means other than fear, I would pass my driving test. One of his first instructions wasn't anything to do with making this metal contraption function, it was to tell me to sit back in my seat, relax my shoulders and release my stranglehold on the steering wheel. It was good advice, even if it had to be reiterated at nearly every lesson.

Uncle Ted was very good at his job, but he had some funny, set ways that I didn't always agree with, particularly because my seat was the one nearest the other traffic on the road.

'Keep out!' he would holler at me, as I persisted in trying to hug the kerb for safety.

'If you hit that kerb, you'll be bounced straight into the cars coming towards you!' He thought I couldn't hear the added, very much quieter, muttering that my scraping along in the gutter wasn't doing his tyres any good either.

There are one or two narrow bridges around where we live and there was one that he insisted was wide enough for two cars to pass over at the same time. Technically, he was correct, but if I had a tape measure, I could guarantee that the distance between each car was definitely putting the safety of the wing mirrors in jeopardy. Maybe he didn't hold as much affection for his wing mirrors as he did for his tyres.

I used to dread approaching this particular bridge as I have always believed that discretion is the better part of valour, politeness costs nothing, more haste, less speed, manners maketh man—and any other axioms that would have given me an excuse to let me sit safely on my side of the bridge and wait whilst the other driver had precedence over me, then I could have had the bridge all to myself and I could have crept over it in my own time, in my own space.

'Keep going, lass, keep going! There's plenty of room for two on this bridge, keep going!' would be ringing in my ears, as I could see the whites of the other driver's eyes, glaring at me in disbelief, as we drew parallel, only inches apart on the brow of the bridge. To this day, I am convinced that Uncle Ted did it for effect, to toughen up his pupils and divide the brave from the pathetic, but he was an excellent teacher, even if his derisive opinion of the other road users was frequently broadcast out of his open window, with great volume but very little tact and diplomacy.

Nowadays, every time I sit, politely waiting for an approaching car to come over to my side of that same bridge, before I take my turn, I can still hear his voice echoing in my head.

'Keep going, lass, keep going, there's plenty of room for two!'

I eventually got the hang of doing six different things with my eyes, feet, and hands, whilst simultaneously aiming a couple of tons of metal so as to avoid colliding with all the other lumps of metal on the road, and Uncle Ted announced it was time to apply for my driving test. It was January 1979 and the weather was foul. I had spent the predictable sleepless night before, going over everything that may or may not happen the following day, but I got through my preliminary lesson with no mishaps. During the last ten minutes of my lesson, as I was driving towards the test centre in Preston, the sky became darker and heavier and, as the centre loomed into sight, it started to snow. My nerves were really kicking in at this point and I couldn't believe that I was going to have to take a driving test with extra complications to add to my anxieties.

We sat and waited in the waiting area, ready to be called through by the examiner. After what seemed like an age, the examiner came through and called my name. I stood up with much trepidation, only to be told that, because the snow had now started to cover up the road markings, all tests were cancelled for the next couple of hours and I would have to re-book. I was aghast that I had gone through so much preparatory apprehension, only to have the test cancelled right at the last minute. Those were the days when appointments were kept, promises were honoured, plans were executed, and schedules were more or less guaranteed, so it was very rare that such an important event did not happen when it should have done.

It was March before I was re-scheduled by the test centre, but the night before this test didn't fill me with dread, the way it had done in January. I was two and a half months more pregnant than I had been in early January and the relaxing hormones had ramped up. I was chilled and ready for anything. I was prepared to be sent away again, in case some other problem arose, so my nerves were completely under control. I completed my lesson beforehand, waited in the test centre until the examiner came to get me, and calmly slid into the seat next to the guy who was going to test my competence, or otherwise.

Well, I say, 'slid into the seat.'

The examiner only noticed my shape when we were walking out to the car and he asked me to read a vehicle number plate at however many yards away was the statutory distance. (You can see I had learnt all the information I needed to know, can't you?) As I carefully negotiated my nearly six-month pregnant, lumbering frame awkwardly around the car door and tried to fit all my bumps and bulges into the driver's seat, without too much overhang, he was looking pointedly at the very close proximity between the steering wheel and the casing over my wriggling infant, and he started to look slightly apprehensive.

Although the wearing of seatbelts wasn't actually obligatory yet, all recent cars had been fitted with them and the Government had been encouraging people to 'Clunk, Click every trip' for some years.

'Well, Mrs Parkinson,' he started nervously. 'Normally, at this stage, I would invite you to ensure that your seatbelt is securely fastened before we commence the test, but I can see that... er... you are erm... Do you want to wear a belt or would you be more comfortable without?' he finished, anxiously.

I assured him that it was probably beyond the capabilities of the said belt to stretch sufficiently around my girth. This was in the days of fixed length seat belts and there was only so much adjustment one could expect from a standard fitment. He seemed relieved that he wasn't going to have to participate in some undignified shuffling about, in a combined effort to persuade an inadequate length of synthetic fibre to locate itself somewhere in a dark recess that couldn't actually be seen. I could also see his mind already fast forwarding to the possible consequences of a heavily pregnant lady being commanded to execute an emergency stop, with a restraining device designed to lock on impact, being fixed around a critical area and him wondering whether he wanted to take the responsibility of premature labour being induced on his shift. I decided to put him out of his misery and leave the seatbelt where it was.

The test proceeded without incident and was very straightforward. I even managed to complete my bête noir—reversing around a corner—with precision and aplomb. The only reason I was able to do this was because Uncle Ted had his Gideon self-adhesive badge fixed exactly in the middle of his car rear window and, during the driving lessons, he used to instruct his pupils precisely which point of the kerb to visually line up with his Gideon badge at which stage, whilst completing the manoeuvre. It was fool-proof and worked every time. The only problem with that form of learning was, when I drove our own car forever after, I was completely useless at reversing around corners because I did not own a Gideon badge.

We arrived back at the driving test centre, and we both emerged from the car, the examiner looking visibly relieved. He beamed at me as he pronounced that I had passed my test and was fit to be let loose on the general public. He didn't actually say the last bit, but I think that was probably one of only a handful of occasions when the examiner was more relieved than the pupil that the driving test was over without any unplanned drama.

CHAPTER 13

Only Yesterday

*It seemed like only yesterday that I was
in the delivery suite first time around*

My second pregnancy was nowhere near as dramatic as the first one, apart from having to be admitted to the antenatal ward to have the baby turned round. My instinct had already told me that I was having a girl, but there were still no scans available for normal pregnancies. I was coming up to my due date, this baby was lying transverse and it is a known medical fact that there is no way babies can be born sideways.

Having a baby turned is a very uncomfortable procedure because the clinicians involved have one goal in mind and that is to turn that baby, come what may. The fact that the fleshy area surrounding the baby belongs to a living, breathing person with pain receptors is forgotten in the focus of the process and the amount of pushing and depth of pressure applied has to be experienced to be believed.

They eventually decided she had been turned into the correct, head-down position to be born naturally, and I was allowed to go home. A couple of days later, whilst trying to rest a cup of tea on my bump without having it heaved off, I realised that I could, once again, feel a bottom and a head, either side of my tummy.

A week after my due date had passed, I was starting to dread a repeat performance of having to go in to hospital to be induced, but thankfully, I woke up about 3:00 am one morning, to the rumblings of labour pains. At least, I assumed that's what they were, as I wasn't familiar with a gradual build-up of contractions. Philip's milk round alarm went off shortly after I had woken up and I informed him that today could well be the day. He did what anyone would do in response to such a momentous announcement— he went to make a cup of tea.

Having established that I didn't look like someone who was going to give birth imminently, whatever one of those looked like, he decided he would go and do his milk round as usual, and he would get back home in a few hours. He had called in at his mum's house, where he kept a big fridge and other supplies and, in the hope of speeding the job up, he dug his youngest brother out of bed to go along and help. The 'help' turned out to involve his barely 13-year-old brother driving the milk van slowly along the roads next to the pavements, keeping pace with Philip who was running alongside, grabbing milk bottles and leaving them on the doorsteps of the terraced houses all down the street. In those days, just about everyone had their milk delivered and the milkmen had their own defined areas, so a lot of milk could be delivered in a relatively short time, especially to the houses which had no garden paths to run up and down.

When one road was completed, Philip would jump back into the van, onto the passenger seat, and his brother continued to drive around the corner to the next street. On one occasion, on rounding the corner, they both spied a police car parked up. Without a word, the van was brought to a halt, he and his brother both jumped out, deposited the next few bottles on the appropriate doorsteps and jumped back into the van, reversing their positions, still not saying a word to each other and Philip drove off, out of sight of the police car.

On completion of his deliveries, he called back at home for a progress report. In the meantime, I had called the delivery unit and the midwife I had spoken to said I should have some breakfast, and then go to the ward. We all had our breakfast and made plans. David was going to stay at his grandma's house and Philip needed to take his milk van back there anyway, so it was decided that Philip would drive his van, I would drive our car with David in the back seat, and little brother would come with me for moral support. Quite what he would have done if a crisis had arisen, I'm not sure. Probably have hopped into the driver's seat and driven me to hospital himself, no doubt.

Driving a car whilst in labour does not make for the easiest journey, not to mention the fact that I was a fairly new driver. There had been no paragraph on contingencies for labour and childbirth in the Highway Code, I was certain of that, but, undeterred, the plan went ahead. The hairiest point came when I had a very strong contraction just as I was negotiating the sharp left turn at Broughton crossroads. Gritting my teeth and forging on, we got everyone to where they should be and Philip and I then went to the antenatal ward, clutching my pre-packed suitcase.

I spent the rest of the day being prodded and poked in the usual places, and then on one visit, the nurse casually remarked that it was very likely that this baby would have to be born by Caesarean section because it was still sideways, just before exiting the room and leaving me to stew over the bombshell she had just dropped.

In 1979, it was still considered that babies would come when they were ready, so no one was in any rush to hurry things along. Philip had gone home to get some sleep and, because I was on the GP-led maternity unit, my family doctor visited that evening to stroke my hand and recommend that I take two paracetamol tablets, so I could get some sleep.

I would like to take this opportunity to state that paracetamol is vastly overrated.

I think most ladies who have ever given birth would agree with me that paracetamol is as much use as the contraceptive pill at that stage, so, unsurprisingly, I didn't get any sleep.

I was determined that I would never again have any pain relief in labour because of my horrible vomiting experience first time round. Around 11:30 pm, I felt things were gaining momentum and I rang for the nurse and asked her to telephone my husband, so he could come in. Husbands in a labour ward were still considered a hindrance and were only tolerated under sufferance, so she scoffed at the idea that we would be needing one of those and told me I was nowhere near ready to give birth.

I insisted that something was going on that hadn't been going on earlier, so she had a quick inspection of the business end. Her face changed, and she said to the student midwife who was accompanying her that she might just want to ring the husband after all—oh, and would she go and find a wheelchair. We would be needing it to get me down the corridor to the delivery room.

Philip arrived in time but the midwife, who had managed to don her delivery gown, only got chance to put on one glove before she needed to catch the rapidly emerging baby who, at some point in the afternoon or evening, had turned herself the right way round again. Everything was straightforward with this delivery and Esther Elisabeth made her way into the world on the 18th of July at 12:35 am. Although she was still eight days overdue, she was the only one of my babies who didn't need inducing. She did it herself, and her regular utterance as a very young child, whenever someone tried to help her with anything was, 'Do it self!'

In sharp contrast to my first postnatal experience when everything was drug-induced confusion and fogginess, this time, I was on a high. I felt like everything was buzzing and I could not get to sleep for about three days. I was elated that we had a little girl. We were so convinced first time round that we were having a boy, and we would call him David James, after both our dads, and now we had a little girl to balance everything off, so both pregnancies had resulted in exactly what we wanted.

I couldn't help feeling we were rather good at this.

The midwives used to visit regularly once you were back at home, and they were very attentive and supportive. There was one older, more old-fashioned midwife who, although she did her job really well, drove me nuts with one particular habit she had. She would come in and insist on waking Esther up, even if she had only just settled, and strip her off completely to check her over and weigh her. She would take off her towelling nappy, which would always be just wet enough not to be able to be put back on, but dry enough to have lasted another two or three hours.

I had learnt a clever way of folding nappies for tiny babies, which resulted in a smaller triangular shape but with an extra padded area down the middle, where it was needed. This smaller version fit a newborn a lot better and I always used a disposable nappy liner strip which could be flushed down the toilet if it got soiled. There were a couple of other methods in nappy folding but I always found them to result in a nappy that was too big in the first few weeks.

This particular midwife would do all she needed to do with Esther, then she would fold a clean terry nappy corner to corner to make a massive, upside down triangle. She would then place the baby on top of the nappy and bring one layer of the bottom point up over the front, then bring each side corner of the triangle down between the legs and tuck the ends inside right next to the functioning part of her bottom. The second layer of the front point would then be brought up to envelope everything, which she would tuck in, secure firmly with a nappy pin from a left-handed direction, dress Esther completely, minus the waterproof pants and rock her happily back to sleep. She would then thrust the baby cheerily into my arms and leave, promising to come back and do it all over again the next day.

I was always left with a dilemma. Did I undress the now sleeping infant in order to rectify the peculiar nappy arrangement and put the very necessary waterproof pants back on, thereby waking up a sleeping baby and possibly wasting another barely damp nappy? The alternative option was to leave things as they were and risk a horrendous fight later with a soiled nappy, the contents of which would have already seeped through all her clothing and carrycot bedding. This nappy would also have a heavily soiled outer front section, two separate corner points to pull out that would be completely covered with whatever had been evacuated, plus the inner front section would have had the benefit of the majority of the onslaught and would defy any strength of Napisan, subsequently remaining stained forever.

It was a dilemma I could have done without as I beamed at the retreating, waving midwife, thanking her profusely and telling her how much I was looking forward to her visit tomorrow, whilst toying with the idea of just cutting the towelling nappy up the sides in order to remove it without splattering a significant area of my carpet with the contents of what was going to be the worst nappy of the day, later on.

That midwife clearly loved her job.

I remember when Esther was about six weeks old. She was in her baby chair in the living room and I had been baking in the kitchen. David was about seventeen months old, and he was toddling about between the two rooms. I had nipped out of the back door to put some rubbish in the outside bin, when David pushed the door shut behind me and started playing with the bolt at the bottom. It happened so fast and by the time I turned around to go back in the house, he had pushed the bolt home, and I was on the wrong side of a locked door.

To say I felt panicked would be an understatement. I had a tiny baby in a seat on the floor, a target for whatever the toddler may decide to bash her on the head with. The same toddler had the free run of the kitchen and knew how to climb on chairs to get what he wanted. I had cakes in the oven, which, if not removed within the next ten minutes would surely start to burn and then it would only be a matter of time before my house would burn down. I have always been an expert in catastrophizing.

I spent quite a few minutes trying to persuade David to undo the bolt, whilst consoling myself that if he was trying to wrestle with a bolt, he couldn't be baby bashing and playing with the sharp knives at the same time. I was getting nowhere fast and my cakes were browning more each minute. Thankfully, because I had cakes in the oven, I had also opened the kitchen window as the room used to get quite steamy with the heat. Thinking quickly, I remembered I had a neighbour across the road, whom I didn't really know that well but I knew she was in possession of at least one small child. I knew her small child was bigger than my small child and, if he could be persuaded to squeeze through my tiny top opener in the window, he might have the understanding and strength to pull the bolt back.

I dashed across the road, knocked on her back door and gabbled out my predicament. She had several small people to choose from, so she grabbed a window-sized one and hauled him back over the avenue to my house. Between us, we posted the heroic young boy through the small opening, and he landed with a bit of a thud and a splash, right in the middle of my quite considerable washing up pile that was in the sink directly below the window, and was liberally coated with various colours and flavours of greasy cake mixture.

With much cajoling and repeated instruction from his mother, the little boy managed to draw the bolt back, and we were able to open the door with great relief. By this time, it had dawned on David that something was very much amiss and that he was on one side of the door, and I was on the other and, what's more, a strange person had just dropped through the kitchen window.

He started to bawl, Esther was already red in the face from her crying that had been going on for the last ten minutes, there was a decidedly smoky aura filling the room, and I was trying to show my profuse gratitude to my new-found friend and her little boy.

It was one way to meet your neighbours but I'm sure there are better ways.

This kind lady came to my rescue on the occasion of another emergency a couple of months later. I promise I did speak to her at other times. She was besotted with my girl baby because she had produced four boys and was always asking if she could babysit Esther for me. She nearly got the chance one day. I had returned from a toddler group late one morning and, to put David on until lunchtime because I had to feed Esther first, I gave him an apple. He loved apples. His first word was *bapoo* (apple, obviously). He was only a couple of bites in when he started to choke—really choke. He could not get his breath, and he was starting to turn blue. I did all the usual things and even tipped him upside down and held him by his ankles but nothing was shifting this piece of apple.

Philip was at home, catching up on his sleep after doing his morning milk round, so he was alerted, I grabbed Esther and ran over the road, thrust her at the startled neighbour who was in her garden and dashed back to the car that Philip had started to reverse out of the drive. Now, this was probably one of the very few occasions when *not* using a child seat saved a toddler's life.

We did have a car seat for David and straps for the carrycot, which we used regularly, but they were not compulsory in those days. It was still okay to sit on the back seat and hold your child on your knee.

Whilst I had dashed over the road with Esther, Philip had put David on the back seat, lying him down because, by now, he was starting to lose consciousness. I opened the back door to jump in next to David to try and revive him during the three-minute dash around the corner to the A & E department. I got in too quickly and, instead of landing next to him, I sat down hard on top of his foot. I don't know how it happened but the pain of having his foot sat on made David react in such a way that the apple piece was dislodged and when he screamed the offending blockage shot out across the car at a rate of knots.

I cannot describe the relief and David and I both sat in the back seat of the car and cried for quite some time, although his reason was entirely different to mine. He was so cross that I had hurt his foot, which, I have to say, remained distinctly bruised for several days, and he wanted his apple back, thank you very much: he hadn't finished it.

My neighbour in crisis was hugely disappointed that she didn't get to keep a girl baby for the afternoon and reluctantly handed Esther back when I went to explain properly what had gone on. She, of course, was pleased that it had all turned out okay but still would have liked some baby-cooing time.

CHAPTER 14

For All We Know

*When we thought we knew where
life was going*

The kitchen in our first house was a tiny, galley shape with a sink under the window and just enough room for a free-standing cooker next to it, squeezed into the corner against the back wall of the house. The opposite long wall had space for a free-standing cupboard with a work top and a tall, narrow fridge freezer. The back door was on the side of the house and led out onto the drive.

Between the sink and the back door was a small area which just about accommodated a twin tub washing machine but it could not be plumbed in where it stood. On wash days, this splendid washing machine had to be pulled away from the wall and the water pipes were attached to the taps in the kitchen sink in order to fill it up with water. For those folk who don't know what a twin tub is, it was a powered washing machine that had two tubs within it. There was a good-sized, stainless steel tub with an automated paddle down the centre. The machine was filled with water and washing powder, plugged in and left to heat up for a while. All the loads used the same water, so things that needed washing on a hot wash or the whites, were dropped in from the top of the washer, and it was switched on and left, with the lid down, for the amount stated on the machine. It only took about twenty minutes then you opened the lid and all the steam came out to meet you. An essential piece of equipment with a twin tub was a pair of long, wooden tongs. The tongs were used to fish around in the water and haul the wet, soapy washing out and transfer it all to the other tub. This doubled up as a rinser and a spinner. There was a handheld hose which was used to manually pour clean water over the washing and this needed doing several times to rinse everything properly, then you could switch the spinner on and it would whizz everything round to extract the water. It was basically handwashing without having to physically agitate and squeeze the laundry yourself, but it was still very hard, manual work. It was also very dangerous because if you lifted the spinner lid and reached in too soon before it had stopped, it could take your arm off. That's if you hadn't already scalded yourself on the red hot water in the other side whilst you were transferring the soapy washing over.

I had two babies in terry nappies so this machine was dragged out most days, which left about six inches of room in the kitchen to get past to reach the kettle. The completed laundry was either pegged out in the back garden or dried on an airer in front of the gas fire.

As soon as our credit card allowed, we progressed to a fully automatic washing machine. We still didn't have the room or facility to plumb it in properly, but we adapted and lengthened the inlet pipes, so they could cope with the machine having to be dragged out regularly. I don't know if you have ever had to lug a washing machine in and out of a confined space several times a week, but it does not do one's back any favours. The very, very important drawback of this new washer was that it was imperative that the U-shaped drainage pipe was hooked over the kitchen sink *before* the washer was switched on and allowed to go through its cycle.

One day, Philip had a couple of free hours, so we decided to go for a trip out to the Trough of Bowland. We wanted to make a picnic of it but it wasn't in summer, so we thought we would go in the Honda pickup milk van which had a flat back to it. There were even fabric sides to make it cosy whilst we sat outside but still up and off the ground on the back of the van.

We had virtually arrived at our destination, which was probably thirty or so minutes away, with David wedged on the van seat between me and Philip, Esther firmly grasped on my knee, and the dog trying to find some room on the very small floor, when I suddenly remembered. As well as packing up a picnic and drinks for us all, I had had the bright idea of putting the washer on to do a load whilst we were all out. It was only at that point that I realised I had not hooked the draining hose over the kitchen sink and it was still coiled up nicely at the back of the machine.

I looked at my watch. The washing machine was ten minutes away from decanting its contents all over the kitchen floor.

A few months before, we had put down brand new carpet tiles to make the hard floor warmer and softer for crawling and playing toddlers and I could already visualise my nice, new floor covering, soaking up the 60°, smelly, soapy outpouring that had just extracted the detritus from eighteen towelling nappies. It was scant consolation that the carpet tiles would also be getting three rinses and a dose of fabric conditioner within the next hour, but there was little point in turning around and heading home now, the damage would have already been done.

We carried on with our picnic, although it wasn't quite the relaxing afternoon I had anticipated, with the looming prospect of what would greet us on our return home. We fully expected that there would be water flowing out on to the drive from under the back door, but we needn't have worried about that.

The angle of the kitchen floor had encouraged the dirty water to flow away from the back door and out of the kitchen in the other direction, into the hall, where the carpet that we were still paying instalments for had soaked up everything that had headed its way.

We hoped against hope that our floor coverings were robust enough to cope with the odd drop of water, but, over the next few days the very unpleasant smell that we had to live with, as the carpet coverings started to dry out, couldn't be ignored. When the carpet tiles all curled up at the edges and the hall carpet shrank away from the skirting boards, we had to concede that we probably should contact the insurance company.

One of the advantages of paying insurance premiums in the early 1980s was that, if you made a claim, it was more than likely to be honoured and you didn't have to spend the next two years fighting your corner. Consequently, a representative called to inspect, sniff, and measure the damage we had incurred. It was deemed that the carpet tiles were beyond redemption and would have to be replaced with new ones, but the hall carpet, because it was only affected at one end, would be professionally cleaned and stretched. Remarkably, the professional attention had the desired effect, although I was always convinced there was a slight whiff of ammonia remaining, every time I passed through the doorway into the kitchen.

I never forgot to hang the drain hose over the sink again.

In 1980, things were getting quite tight, money-wise. Our trusty credit card could only do so much and, however we tried to work things out, there was more money going out than there was coming in and that is never a happy situation.

Philip changed jobs early that year and went to work in an agricultural supplies firm as a milking machine engineer. The work was completely new to him, and he was working as part of a team of mechanical fitters. The first time he went on to a farm, he managed to set himself alight with sparks from the angle grinder he was using. His boiler suit caught fire in a very embarrassing region of his anatomy, and he had to continue to wear that particular boiler suit for quite some months, complete with a charred-edge hole. He got no sympathy at all but provided a lot of entertainment for the farmer.

Although he was enjoying the challenge, the salary was quite basic, so we were still keeping our options open. We looked into the possibility of buying a Post Office. I don't know whether the process is the same today, but back then, you applied to be a Sub-postmaster/mistress, as you would any other job, then waited to hear from Head Office. If you had been selected for a preliminary interview, you had to be able to demonstrate that, not only were you suitable for the job, but you were also in a favourable position to be able to buy the house or dwelling that the sub-post office was located in. In order to be prepared for that eventuality, we hunted for post offices for sale, in the local paper's Businesses For Sale section, and went and viewed, as you would a house, but it would also be to assess the business options. It was a complicated procedure because the house had to suit your requirements with size, location, price and everything you look for in a new house, but the business had to be making the profit margins needed to sustain a viable living. Invariably, there would be a shop of some description to complement the post office side of things, so there was an awful lot to consider. It was an 'all or nothing' venture.

At the time, we were quite convinced that our path in life was heading for post office ownership, so we put our house in Fulwood up for sale. We had only just completed the refurbishment of the last room, but at least it looked good for any prospective buyers. It sold remarkably quickly and very early in 1981, we found ourselves imminently homeless, but with the deposit available to put down on a property if necessary, on the brink of a new venture.

We had looked at Galgate post office near Lancaster and Friargate post office in Preston town centre, but neither of those were quite the property we wanted as a family home. They both were tall buildings with cellars and were quite formidable-looking buildings. We looked at Houghton post office and Croston, both of which had cottages attached that appealed to us, but either way, we would be moving out of our familiar home setting. We decided to apply for Philip to become a sub-postmaster with the Croston property in mind. He went through all the processes and interviews and it was all looking very likely that we were heading to the southern end of the county to live. Right at the last possible minute, word came back from Head Office to say that he had just been pipped at the post, but if he would like to apply again if another opening came up, he would almost certainly be offered a position.

At the time we were quite devastated as all the signs had pointed in one direction. I had even measured up for curtains for the lovely house in Croston. We had prayed about the new venture and were convinced that this was the right direction for us to move in. It was a long time later when we found out that in the ensuing years, all of the properties we had considered buying had subsequently suffered huge amounts of damage due to flood waters encroaching into the premises during one storm or other, and all of the post offices and staff had been held up at gunpoint at various times. I'm not sure I could have coped with that!

We don't always have the privilege of seeing the benefits of God's protective hand on us as we go through life, but, as always, He knew what He was doing when He guided us in that particular venture.

By this time, we had had to move out of our home in Fulwood and our only option, until we found somewhere else to live, was to move to Philip's mum's house in Woodplumpton and live in our caravan for a few months. This sounds fairly straightforward, but there were four of us plus quite a bit of furniture to store, and it was a very cold winter.

We had bought our caravan with some of the proceeds from selling the milk round, despite the fact that I was extremely nervous about being in a car that was towing a caravan.

I had good reason to be. During my teenage years, my parents had decided, one summer, to go on a caravan trip around the Continent (as it was known then) and I had to go with them. They had a touring caravan and a large, substantial VW car with which to tow it, so everything should have gone smoothly. We had travelled for some time, without incident, in a southerly direction towards Dover, in order to catch the ferry. Halfway down the motorway, my mother decided she would take over the driving. Before long, during a particularly protracted downhill stretch, the caravan started to sway. My dad was telling my mother what action she should take to pull out of the sway but his instructions went unheeded. I can still feel the sensation of being in the back of a car that was losing its battle with a weighty trailer which had gained momentum and was now swinging wildly from side to side, taking the car with it. I can tell you, it was certainly the scariest moment of my life up to that point, as we careered off the motorway and down a steep, grassy embankment at breakneck speed, stopping only as we hit the bottom of the bank and the whole unit tipped over onto its side.

Miraculously, no one was seriously injured but the car and caravan were complete write-offs. The RAC came to sort us out and took us to a place to stay overnight whilst we sorted out a replacement vehicle. My dad was taking no more chances as he knew he and my mother would be sharing the driving whilst on foreign soil, so he hired a motor caravan for the rest of the holiday. We went back to the wreckage to retrieve what we could of our equipment and belongings to pack into our alternative accommodation, and there, sitting in a patch of undisturbed grass was a box of eggs which had flown off the rear parcel shelf when the hatchback of the car had burst open during the impact, perfectly intact.

Back in Woodplumpton, the caravan we had bought was only a tourer but it had excellent kitchen facilities and the layout and size made it very workable, apart from the fact that the nights proved too cold and damp for Esther. As a toddler, she suffered from asthma and the atmosphere was too much for her to sleep through most nights without triggering horrible, barking, wheezing attacks.

Although there wasn't a spare bedroom in the main house, everyone was shuffled around and stacked up into fewer bedrooms to release one that we could all sleep in. This room was the one that Philip used before we were married, so he felt right at home. The difference now was that the long narrow room had to accommodate a double bed, a single bed, a cot and a single wardrobe, as well as some of the original furniture, which was too big to move out onto the landing. The restricted space was made even more interesting by the fact that the end wall, which had the beds lined up along it, was only about four feet high because the ceiling sloped down with the angle of the roof and joined with the wall at that side. Our double bed was right up against this wall and Philip got the short straw (or short wall, if you like), and he was the one who had to clamber into place from the open side of the bed and banged his head every time he tried to sit up. It was okay, he was used to it.

Apparently, if ever the doctor visited them when they were children, he would bend over the bed to examine the ailing child and listen to their chest, and every time, without fail, he would crack his head on the ceiling beam when he straightened up. They probably feigned illness just so they could laugh at the doctor banging his head.

That was an interesting few months and not a lifestyle I would be in a rush to repeat. I continued to cook in the caravan kitchen, and we mostly used the caravan as our own private space and went into the house to sleep. We learnt to live life on the edge, and by that I mean that there was no bannister on the landing and no stair rail on the stairs. To get to the bathroom we had to cross a short, narrow walkway that had a sheer, unprotected drop down to the hall below. I slipped down those stairs many a time, trying to juggle two small children and a basketful of dirty washing.

Ironically, the time I really did do myself an injury was when I missed my footing coming out of the caravan one day. The free-standing step slipped and I fell and landed on my wrist. So, a broken wrist and an arm in plaster were added to the mix. If Social Services had got wind of the precarious living arrangements of my kids, I would have been put on a register, for sure.

It was around that time that I realised a very important fact of life.

It is impossible to peel potatoes with one hand.

CHAPTER 15

It's Gonna Take Some Time

Renovating our new house

During the time we lived our itinerant lifestyle, we continued to pursue the idea of buying a post office, but gradually, all our options disappeared for one reason or another so Philip decided to stay put in the job he had, and we started looking for a house we could afford. In the five years' time lapse since we had bought our first house in 1981, house prices had just about tripled. We thought we were well off with the price we had got for our house in Fulwood, but, of course, we were now wanting to buy a house and were going to have to pay a comparable price. We had noticed a semi-detached house in Woodplumpton village had been up for sale for some time. We also noticed that it was in a very poor state. Nevertheless, we made an appointment to have a look around to get an idea of what we would get for our money.

It was a very basic interior when we went inside. The previous occupant had been an old lady and the estate agent was even kind enough to point out exactly where she had died. The house itself was structurally sound, apart from the window frames, which were all stuffed up with bits of carpet and underfelt to stop the draughts, so they would all need replacing. All the floors were constructed from wooden floorboards, apart from the small kitchen floor, which had been concreted and painted but, over time, had developed a curious, cracked hump in the middle. The hilly area covered a significant part of the floor, so that would need smashing up and re-laying.

Next to the back door, taking up at least a third of the area, was a very old-fashioned toilet. It was of the flushing variety but it must have been one of the first of its kind. That would need removing, and the floor and walls re-surfacing.

There was a small, ten-foot square dining room with an open fire grate built across one corner of it. Nice and cosy, I'm sure, but not very safe, given the confined area that the children would be in. That would have to be changed for a stove that would heat the domestic water. The lounge was a reasonable size, very light and bright, with views right across the fields to Blackpool, but we were slightly disconcerted by the one and only electrical socket in the room, which was positioned halfway up the chimney breast and the wallpaper surrounding it was decidedly sooty and singed. Not to worry. That would be rectified when we rewired the whole house.

We went upstairs, to find two double bedrooms, a bathroom, and a boxroom. The bathroom only had an old, cast iron bath and a big porcelain sink, no toilet. That's okay. We would need a new bathroom suite, so we would design it so we could squeeze a toilet in as well. The back bedroom had a good corner of it taken over by a cylinder cupboard but the contents were old and rusty and it was in an odd place. We were unfazed, though, because that could be moved when the whole house was re-plumbed and the new immersion tank and water tank were installed. The front bedroom was, again, bright and had an even better view—this time we could see Blackpool Tower in the distance, miles away across the fields. The crumbling plaster and bricks under the window were not a problem. They could be replaced when the old, open fireplace was blocked up and half the room was re-plastered. The six foot by seven foot boxroom was fine. As long as it was large enough for a cot, whenever would we need to fit a single bed, a wardrobe, half a ton of Lego and a set of drawers in there?

It wasn't all bad news, though. Although every single surface, fitment, fixture, and installation would have to be removed, replaced, re-sited, re-covered, or re-invented, we wouldn't have to worry about the gas supply. There wasn't any.

There was a good-sized back garden with lots of established fruit trees in it and at the far end, there was a dyke with a fast flowing stream running across its width. It wouldn't be much of a problem to prevent a roving toddler from drowning themselves, and, if the escaping child did make it safely across and gain free access to the open fields behind, it would be easy enough to scramble through all the gaps in the holly and hawthorn hedge to retrieve them. We were sure the dilapidated, wooden shed would hold up for at least one more winter, as long as we didn't lean on it too heavily and the massively overgrown hawthorn hedges surrounding the whole perimeter could be tamed if we knew where to source scythes and machetes, and we had a spare week when we had nothing else to do.

It was a bargain.

For the princely sum of £21,500.00, we signed on the dotted line and this money pit became ours. Well, it was Yorkshire Building Society's to be strictly accurate, but they were happy enough to let us live there.

1981 turned out to be quite an historic year in several ways.

Ronald Reagan became the US President in the January, although someone took exception to him and shot him in the March, Charles and Diana got married in the July and it was the year that the Yorkshire Ripper was arrested. It was also the year that we began our long residence in the centre of Woodplumpton Village. At time of writing, we have lived here for nearly 39 years, and there are still jobs we have not managed to get done (but I've been assured that it'll not take him a minute, when he does get around to it).

We spent a couple of months before we moved in, doing a lot of work on the house. Philip re-wired right through, but of course, that involved floor boards being taken up in every room and no wall was left un-gouged, as he channelled through the plaster to create routes for the wires to be installed and, hopefully, all joined up in the right ways. All the old lead pipes had to be ripped out and new, copper ones re-routed and installed. It was almost inevitable that someone would end up standing on one of several large, rusty nails that were protruding from the many upturned floor boards and it turned out to be me. It went right through my shoe and into my foot. Cue a visit to A & E and the administration of a tetanus booster.

During these processes, we discovered that the suspect socket located on the chimney breast in the lounge was, indeed, a potential death trap. All the wires connected to it were black and burnt for a good six inches and, apparently, the next-door neighbour had gone in several times a week to replace the old-fashioned fuses that kept blowing, when the old lady had been alive. Come to think of it, no one ever said what she'd died of. She could have been electrocuted for all we knew.

It would only have been a matter of time, though, before the house could have burnt down for another reason. The open fireplace that was across the corner of the dining room at the back of the house had been built directly on top of the wooden floor boards! The part that actually contained the fire was sat on a concrete base which, in turn, was sat on top of the floor boards. The boards were charred and only partially intact.

We bought a solid fuel stove that would heat the hot water and run several radiators (if we had any), and built a solid, concrete filled, supporting wall up from the foundations under the house to seat it on and trimmed the floor boards out of harm's way.

I loved that stove. It was kept permanently lit with very little effort and I also had a multi-line airer attached to both walls, across the corner above it. My washing dried overnight and it was up and out of the way. It was far more efficient and cheaper than any tumble dryer, although I always coveted one of those old-fashioned, wood and metal airers that operated on a rope and pulley system, which could be lowered to make hanging the washing easier, then hauled up above the room near the ceiling, but our domestic budget did not stretch to such luxuries. Instead, I made do with clambering on and off dining chairs at frequent intervals and having wet washing flapping in my face whilst I tried to reach the furthest extremities of the line without losing my balance.

By the time we moved into our new house on August Bank Holiday weekend in 1981, we had most of the essential amenities installed. When I say 'most', I mean that we had electric light and cold water to the bathroom upstairs. The new toilet wasn't quite plumbed in and the kitchen was completely unusable and mostly consisted of broken lumps of concrete at floor level, with the walls punctuated with bare wires and copper pipe ends, eagerly waiting to be connected up to something else that would render them functional.

Thankfully, we also had an uncle and auntie who lived next door but one, who allowed us to use their bathroom and toilet for as long as was necessary. We didn't have to trouble them much for the use of their toilet as ours was plumbed in successfully within a day, but we did troupe over regularly in the evenings, clutching our toilet bags, shampoo, towels, and pyjamas, in order to get ourselves and the children bathed and hair-washed. Even then, showers were not in standard use and everyone would have rubber shower-headed attachments that you shoved onto the taps, with varying degrees of success, depending on the shape of your taps.

We were not totally bereft of modern conveniences. We had a hosepipe with many, many connectors, to make it long enough to reach from Uncle Stan's outside tap, draped across our neighbour's garden and in at our back door. That was our downstairs water supply. For several weeks, I had to take all the washing down the road to use my mother-in-law's washing machine, but we were okay for cooking and washing up because we had parked our caravan in our new back garden. It was a huge bonus that we had good weather, and we enjoyed a very mild autumn.

A few weeks after moving in, Philip had established a hot water supply to the bathroom, so we felt very well off because we could now bathe ourselves in our very own new bath whenever we wanted, without having to trail through the village. We were very proud of our colour choice of cutting-edge, up-to-the-minute, fashionable, chocolate brown for our bathroom suite. I have to concede that it does not look quite so fashionable at the present time, but it still functions and looks like new, so it is staying, for now. (Quote from the Man of the House: 'There's nothing wrong with it!')

We probably should get an award for having had the best value for money from a 1980s purchase that has been in constant use.

I had borrowed an electric spin dryer, which stood in isolated glory on the only flattish area of kitchen floor we could find, and was attached, by numerous extension leads, to the nearest working electrical socket. Until the kitchen had been renovated and new units fitted though, we still had no washing machine.

I devised quite a system of soaking the double load of towelling nappies every night in the Napisan bucket up in the bathroom. Every morning, I would tip the contents of the bucket into the bath, drain off the murky, smelly water, and add fresh hot water plus washing powder. I would then lift David and Esther into the bath, and they would run up and down on top of everything in their bare feet, agitating the washing and having a great time, whilst I held their hands, I hasten to add.

We would repeat it all a couple of times with rinsing water then let everything drain off. I knew how to provide cheap entertainment, and the rashes they developed from having their delicate baby skin in regular contact with concentrated washing solution had long faded by the time they went to school.

The downside of all this frivolity was that I then had to carry all the heavy, dripping wet washing back downstairs in a large bucket, as well as herd two toddlers around the lifted floorboards with rusty nails, all whilst avoiding splinters on our naked stairs that were booby-trapped with saws, chisels, screwdrivers and the like. I could then load the wet washing, in small amounts, into the top loading spinner. This thing would take off like Concorde but as it gained momentum, it would start to travel across the floor. It was oblivious to the lumps and bumps of the concrete and if you left it unattended for two minutes, it would be in a totally different place, restricted only by its own electrical cord. It had a penchant for the back door and it was only the storm guard at the bottom of the door frame that stopped it walking off into the garden.

My ability to include my neighbours in my domestic predicaments accompanied me to our second house and the lovely lady who lived next door, who already had our hosepipe running across her garden, kindly offered me the use of her washing line whenever I wanted it. The three of us would troop out of our front garden gate and in through hers and back along her path, all carrying something, and we would peg the washing out whilst she was at work and if I didn't get around to gathering it all back in by the time she came home, she would do that for me and bring it round to my house.

My older two children had no need of toys when we first moved into what was little more than a building site. They lived in a chaotic space with all manner of dangerous risks to overcome and, if they had known who Indiana Jones was, in the recently released movie, they could have matched his skills at staying alive under treacherous circumstances without batting an eyelid.

Don't get the wrong idea, though. I did take measures to keep them safe. I always made sure the lounge door was kept closed when they were in there watching children's television when I left them alone in the house to make the evening meal in the caravan kitchen. And they were always nice and warm when they sat, huddled together on the homemade rug, as close as they could get to the open coal fire to avoid the draughts that came up through the floorboards.

Winter was approaching and the novelty of our camping-like experience in our new house had long since worn off. It was imperative to get the old kitchen floor hacked up and a new one laid before any significant progress could be made, so, reinforcements had to be called in, in the guise of two uncles and a couple of brothers.

They all turned up on the appointed day, which was a miracle in itself. They stood round looking at the offending floor and devised a very precise plan as to what would be the most efficient way to contain all the mess, so it didn't encroach into the rest of the house, to get rid of the waste, so we didn't have to live with it piled up against the rickety garage for the next three years and even, discussed, in a most courteous manner, the best way to lay the new floor, each of them respecting another's idea above his own.

Hah! Only kidding.

What actually happened was, each of them grabbed the nearest weapon of mass-destruction to hand and set about the already cracked concrete, with scant regard for the whereabouts of toddlers, dog or niece/sister-in-law, who all had to flee for cover from flying rubble and stay out of harm's way for the rest of the day.

I didn't miss any of the conversation or action, though. The whole house resonated and shook with each thump of the sledgehammers and I could hear every word from the next room, as the 'conversation' got louder and louder as each one wanted his voice heard above the rest. What we ended up with was a crater-like area with no particular consistency in measurement, but with assurances that 'the new concrete will level everything out and it'll be reet'.

I firmly believe that that may have been the case, to some extent, if the concrete had been laid and allowed to set after being levelled out properly. If someone hadn't had the bright idea, the next time they turned up to help, to lay the new ceramic tiles on top of the wet cement, 'to save us another job', instead of laying them properly, with proper adhesive on a nice, flat floor. As it was, it ended up being a race to lay the tiles before the concrete set, with too many legs in the way, and one person hindering another, and all enthusiasm running out seven-eighths of the way through and one person going home before the job was finished and... you get the picture.

How that floor has survived as long as it has is a mystery. Oh wait—it's concreted in.

The new, bargain, end-of-season-sale kitchen units were gradually installed and, finally, on Christmas Eve, I acquired a working kitchen. The fridge was moved from the dining room into its permanent corner in the kitchen, although I still spent all Christmas Day wandering into the dining room on a fool's errand to get the food out of it, and we had the old, second-hand cooker in place and connected into the electric. There was hot water coming out of the brand new mixer tap, and it was only a matter of time before the washing machine would be plumbed in.

There was no paint, or tiling, or plaster, or sealant, or edge trims, or kickboards, or door fronts, but it was such a luxury to have the basic amenities where they should be and (mostly) working, that we thought we were royalty.

We were cosy and warm downstairs that first winter but there was no heating upstairs at all. One or two radiators had been fixed to the wall here and there, but nothing was connected up yet. We had lots of hot water bottles, and plenty of blankets, though, and we had an electric under-blanket on our bed. The window frames were being replaced, so the house was getting more and more secure and weatherproof. It was a bitterly cold winter, and because we were still renovating various rooms, we had random holes in some of the upstairs walls. I remember coming home from church one Sunday evening and dashing straight upstairs to go to the loo, where I was met with a mound of snow in the bathroom. The wind had been blowing from the back of the house and had directed a whole load of snow through the hole where the toilet waste pipe was positioned in the outside wall, and it had not yet been reduced and repointed around.

We were so grateful for the permanently hot Rayburn stove which did a lot to keep the chill off everything until the following winter when the upstairs radiators could be completed and functioning.

CHAPTER 16

Merry Christmas, Darling

Whose idea was it to have a baby due on Christmas Eve?

1982 brought another upheaval in our lives. Looking back, it is remarkable to realise just how many major life changes we had in such a very few years. By the time we had been married six years, we had gone through five different job situations between us, had two babies, and two almost derelict houses to renovate, all whilst carrying on with all the other normal activities of life and being part of all the church events.

We were busy every Sunday, with teaching Sunday School classes and attending twice daily services. We had recently started up a music group which played at some services initially, and progressed and developed into a larger band over the years which played and led the church worship every Sunday evening. I played the violin and Philip played the bass guitar, and the band continued for another three and a half decades.

After settling into his new job as a milking machine engineer the previous year, Philip was approached by his boss, who was the business owner, and asked what he thought of the possibility of taking over the company and buying the boss out when he retired. Given that he was the most junior member of staff, it was a rather surprising proposal, but it was clear that Philip had a flair for the job and had adapted very quickly and was rapidly learning new skills.

After a fair bit of discussion and pondering, Philip and his Uncle Stan, who had lent us his bathroom facilities next door but one, decided to go into business together, and approached the bank for a business loan. So, in January 1982, we took on the ownership of Porter's Agricultural Supplies and life was never the same again.

The business consisted of a well-established agricultural ironmongery shop, situated opposite the entrance of the Cattle Market in Brook Street, Preston, a van sales service, which travelled around the farms of the Fylde selling chemicals and all other sundries that farmers needed, and of course, the engineers, who installed, repaired and maintained the milking machines that milked the dairy cows, and sometimes, goats on the Lancashire farms.

Uncle Stan's domain was the Preston shop and its sister branch at Lancaster Auction Mart. He had no knowledge of the engineering aspect, so he ruled the retail side and soon had things organised as he wanted them.

Philip suddenly found himself in the odd position of instant promotion and was now the boss over all his workmates, but everyone seemed to adapt well, and as long as they got their wages, I don't think there was any resentment. I was introduced into the fascinating (that may be the wrong word) world of manual double-entry bookkeeping and the joys of becoming intimate with massive, lined, accounting ledgers, whose columns of figures always, always ended up one or two pence adrift when the totals were added up. Such was my nature that I always had to find and rectify those one or two pence, even if it took until late into the night. I learnt to work out the weekly wages and National Insurance contributions from the myriad charts and reference tables supplied by the Tax Office and stuff the little brown wage packets with handwritten wage slips and cash.

Sales and Purchase Ledgers, paper invoices, remittance advices, and statements were the stuff of my nightly dreams as I entered a new phase of life that I had not prepared for during my years of education. I had been steered well past the commerce and business courses by my teachers and parents, in favour of the more academic, exam-based lessons, yet here I was, with a whole new vocation to learn from scratch.

To say that Porter's took over our lives is not an exaggeration by any means. Philip was rarely at home, frequently working late or being called out, and nearly every call-out emergency would take longer than it needed to because he was learning on the job all the time. A diagnosis and repair job that would take him half an hour to fettle nowadays, would take two or three hours in those early days because everything was a new experience.

Never, ever, take for granted a professional person's skill and expertise, or begrudge paying them what they charge. Their experience has always been gained through hard work, dedication, and sacrifice—if not their own, then probably their family members'.

There is a well-known anecdote in agricultural circles about an occasion when a farmer was doing what he did best and was querying an invoice that had just been presented to him by a tradesman.

'Ow much?!' he exclaimed. 'Tha's only bin 'ere 10 minutes. What's tha' chargin' for?'

'I charged a fiver for coming out to your farm and tightening that loose connection. The rest of the bill is for 25 years of training and experience to be able to diagnose the problem and knowing where to find the screw that needed tightening,' came the reply of the expert.

Philip was usually unaware of how many children were asleep at our house on any given evening because he would usually come in late, long after the children's bedtime, eat, doze in front of the TV, go to bed, and get up early. If an extra child, who had been sleeping over, appeared at the breakfast table, he would find an extra dish, fill it with cereal, and go back off to work.

It was a surprise to us both, then, that I found out in the early summer that I was pregnant again. This baby was due on Christmas Eve. I had always vowed I would never have a baby around Christmas, because it doesn't seem fair on them for their birthday celebrations, so I was a bit miffed, on behalf of my unborn offspring, for our rubbish timing, but obviously thrilled that we were expecting number three.

We had already arranged to go on holiday to Wales in the summer, with some friends of ours, not realising quite what that meant when you have your own business. In our naivety, we thought we would be able to have holidays when we wanted, for as long as we wanted and all would carry on smoothly back home, with all the willing members of staff taking care of business. Our simplistic bubble was burst very early on in this self-employed status, however, and our holiday was disrupted every other day, when Philip would head back home to keep something ticking over, or avert a crisis at work and I would stay in Wales with two children and our friends for company. It was not the most restful holiday we have ever had, and we probably wouldn't have even attempted to go on vacation, had it not been booked in advance.

Things did not improve when I had some sort of reaction whilst I was there. We were never sure what it was, but my pregnancy caused some extreme sensitivity, possibly to the sun, and I expanded like a Michelin man. Everything swelled to twice its size and I could not lift my arms at all. So, all in all, not a great success, but that holiday rather set the tone for the future and having a business where you are permanently on call does pose some challenges when you want family time off.

The rest of that year was spent adjusting to new work life, home refurbishment and getting our heads around the fact that Britain was at war with Argentina over ownership of the Falkland Islands. The news channels spoke of little else, other than the birth of Prince William, who was born just after the Falklands war ended. Although this war did not affect the daily life of the average person living in the UK, the vast television coverage of all the activity was quite unsettling.

As the end of the year approached, I was not going to be caught out by the small inconvenience of having a baby in the middle of all the festivities, so, by mid-November, I was sorted. I had bought every present, written every card, made and iced the Christmas cake, and got everything ready for our new member of the family who would be joining us.

I also managed to almost get myself arrested in Marks and Spencer's during my preparations. I had been Christmas shopping and, as well as having my own shopping bags, I had been handed my purchases in some more carrier bags when I was at the till. I was struggling to keep hold of everything, as well as keeping a firm grip on Esther, and checking where David was, so I wanted to amalgamate my purchases into fewer bags. I found myself a quiet corner and started to transfer items from the store carrier bags into my own. I had only been there less than a minute, when an over-en-thusiastic security guard appeared and loomed over me, asking me what I thought I was doing. I explained that I was struggling with my shopping and was only trying to redistribute my load.

He gave me a good telling off and told me to stop doing what I was doing because it looked very suspicious and told me to be on my way. If I hadn't been so full of pregnancy hormones and had two small children about to witness everything I said, I would have given him a piece of my mind and suggested that perhaps he would have been better occupied actually helping an eight-month pregnant lady, rather than acting like an insensitive chauvinistic pi— person!

As it was, I burst into tears, left the shop and went straight home, vowing to myself that I would never go into that store ever again. Of course, I did go there again—it was Marks and Spencer's after all—but I always felt rather guilty and that I was being watched.

I was on edge all that Christmas, waiting to go into labour at any minute, but it was not to be. The day after Boxing Day, I phoned a friend of mine who was also due at the same time and had an antenatal appointment on the same day as me. I was only ringing her to offer her a lift to the hospital, but I was very disappointed to learn from her husband, who answered the house landline, that she would not be coming with me after all, because her baby had been born on time, and she was now on the right side of it all. I was, of course delighted for her as I made my weary, lonesome way to the clinic to be prodded and assessed, then went back home again, to wait, and wait, and wait.

I was finally admitted to the antenatal ward on New Year's Eve, with the promise that I would be induced.

'Great', I thought. 'There's a chance we might get our photo in the local paper, as one of the mums with New Year babies'.

But that was not to be, either. I was gazumped. A lady who was expecting twins and was having difficulties was given preference over me. Honestly, some people will go to any lengths to push in. Or push out, in her case. I bet she got her photo in the local paper.

I spent that New Year's Eve feeling very sorry for myself and listening to the nurses giggling in the ward office as they partied surreptitiously with the odd tot of festive lemonade.

I'm not sure what happened to the 1st, 2nd and 3rd days of January, because the doctor with the magic pessary only got around to me on the 4th of January. Once things got going however, they moved on apace and I caught the midwives napping again, which meant there was no time to get me up to the delivery suite. I was manoeuvred into the treatment room off the antenatal ward, where our third baby was born just before 4:00 pm, complete with the membranes intact—known as 'en caul'—which is a very rare thing.

He shared his now-redundant living quarters with all the staff as the membranes had to be physically broken and all the amniotic fluid gushed out over everyone's shoes, but nobody minded. If you are superstitious, it's supposed to mean that the baby will be lucky in life when they are born with the amniotic sac intact and that they will never be drowned at sea.

Good to know.

I was transferred upstairs to the GP Unit shortly afterwards and allowed home the next day. There was a new scheme being trialled, whereby you were allowed to go home earlier than had previously been allowed, but you went by hospital transport and a midwife followed on and would arrive at your home at the same time. It sounded like an excellent plan, but in reality it was a nightmarish journey. Three or four of us new mums were escorted to a freezing cold, sitting ambulance, still in our nighties, slippers and dressing gowns in the middle of winter and clutching our brand new infant who was wrapped up in a blanket. I was also trying to keep track of an overnight case, a bunch of flowers, and various other bits and bobs, because I had already been in hospital for several days.

The seats in the ambulance were fixed along the sides of the vehicle, so you sat facing inwards, opposite the other passengers. There were no seat belts and because they were bench-type seats, there was nothing to anchor you sideways either.

This ambulance had four of us to drop off at our respective homes and, of course, my home was the furthermost out, so I got to experience the maximum length of the journey. We travelled all round Ashton, Fulwood, and Ingol and every time we went round a corner, we were either thrown forward into the aisle or rammed back into our bench seat. We were each clutching a baby and of course, not feeling at our peak, balance-wise, anyway.

There was nothing to grab hold of and even I, with my long legs, could only just touch my toes on the opposite bench seat, if I slid my bottom forward on my seat as far as was safe, to try to get an anchor to steady myself. It was nothing short of dangerous in the extreme. I cannot imagine who could ever have thought of such a mode of transport for anyone who had full strength and all their limbs available, never mind ill, disabled, or vulnerable patients. There was a definite irony, in that the law making it obligatory for all car drivers and passengers to wear seat belts came into force later that month on the 31st of January. I think, though, it was still many more years before bus or communal passengers were required to wear seat belts.

I have never been so relieved to have sight of my own front door in my life, and I was shaking as I left that ambulance. The midwife pulled up in her car at the same time, but I've no idea whether she had also taken the scenic route behind the ambulance, or not. I can't help thinking there were multiple flaws in this new, postnatal scheme they were trialling, but I don't suppose it lasted very long anyway. The GP Unit and the old Preston Royal Infirmary closed down soon after that and all PRI maternity services were combined with the rest of the obstetrics department at Sharoe Green Hospital in Fulwood.

However, it was lovely having the midwife looking after everything and when she had finished all her checks, I was told to go to bed and stay there until she came again later in the day.

She visited twice a day for the first three days, then once a day up until the tenth day, and then two more visits, bringing it up to the fourteenth day. We were well looked after, although she didn't make meals, which was a bit of a disappointment.

The day I was discharged back home was David's first day at school. The school entry for infants was split into two intakes per school year at that time, to spread the load of new pupils, so there weren't too many new children starting all at once and the younger half could commence their school year in the January term.

I say, 'spread the load'.

For Woodplumpton Primary School, this involved less than a dozen children, but they still had to split the intake in line with the rest of the county, to give parents the option.

In any family, it is quite a momentous occasion when the firstborn starts school, but in our family, it wasn't quite so straightforward. Because the baby had delayed his arrival until the year after he was due (and has been late for most things ever since) there were too many things happening at the same time to be able to appreciate each event individually. David had been taken to school in the morning, but I hadn't been the one to get him dressed in his carefully prepared uniform and wave him off at the school gates for the first time. Nor did I go and pick him up after his first day and listen to first day experiences on the walk home. It was a bitter-sweet experience, because he rushed into the house and straight upstairs when he was brought home and was so excited to see his new baby brother for the first time. Although he wasn't exactly a chatterbox normally, he didn't know what to say first, so his eager attempts to fill me in on everything that had happened that day came out in a rush of garbled words that fell over themselves.

When the midwife came to visit us on the fourteenth day, I shared my concerns with her about my new baby. He had steadily been retaining fluid since his birth and was now looking decidedly puffy and swollen all over. After briefly examining him, she made arrangements to have him admitted to the Children's Ward at Preston, immediately. We took him in late afternoon, where, of course there was a lot of form filling.

The first thing they asked us was his name. What was he called?

We looked at each other and didn't quite know how to answer. We had spent the last two weeks trying to make our minds up for definite because we had a difference of opinion. I wanted to call him Matthew, with possibly Dawson as a middle name because we both had that name in our families, but Philip was more in favour of Philip. Although I liked the name very much, I said it would cause confusion, having two Philips in the family, but Philip didn't think it would be a problem. We had agreed on William as a middle name, because that was one of my dad's names and it had been Philip's grandad's name.

The paediatric nurse was hovering, pen in hand, looking from one to the other of us. She had other things to be getting on with—how hard was it to name your child, for goodness sake? We hurriedly decided, as her hand was lowering towards the admissions sheet.

Philip William it was. He had been admitted to the ward, and he was official. No going back now. He was given a perfunctory examination by the junior doctor on duty, and we were told to stay in overnight, and he would be seen properly in the morning, on the ward round. Only one parent was allowed to stay, but we were very fortunate to be in a brand new building, part of the Royal Preston Hospital, that had only been built recently, and it had been a revolutionary decision to attach some rooms to the children's ward, where mums could stay overnight.

The official opening ceremony of the hospital was to take place in June that year, and Princess Diana was booked to do the honours.

The nurses were very kind, although Philip Junior was put into a full-sized cot, which looked ridiculous for a two-week-old baby. He was not concerned about his own condition, although he was very sleepy and slightly lethargic, but because he was not causing any alarm, the nurses told me to go and get some sleep, and they would come and get me when he needed feeding. It's a strange thing, sitting by the side of the cot of a tiny baby, who is an inpatient. There's not a lot of conversation, they don't appreciate grapes and reading books to them is largely a wasted occupation because they are asleep. Cuddling your baby unnecessarily was not encouraged and, unless you were feeding or changing your baby, they had to be put back behind the bars, so to speak.

As promised, the Senior Doctor entered the ward at the appointed time the following day, with his entourage of medical students, like a ship in full sail followed by a flotilla of tiny vessels. His white coat flapped wide in the breeze created by the speed of his walk, and he clearly wanted to give the impression that he owned that particular section of the hospital. His speedy progress came to an abrupt halt when he reached our bay but the convoy behind him didn't stop quite as smartly, so there was a fair bit of careering around on the back row of the dozen or so students as they tried, but failed, to look nonchalant and professional.

I, as the patient's mother, was given a polite, 'Good morning, Mother,' then the doctor invited several students to examine the placid little figure lying in the cot. They were mostly scared stiff of both their boss and the patients, but one or two of the students waved their stethoscopes in the general direction of my baby, then scuttled back to a safe distance, so they wouldn't be picked on to comment or answer any questions.

'Well?' the physician bellowed, sweeping his glare across the assembled group.

'Has anybody got an opinion about this little chap?' There was silence and a lot of shuffling of feet.

'Can no one offer a possible diagnosis as to the cause of this oedema?'

There was a hand half-raised from the back row, and a timid voice piped up, 'Could it be heart failure, Sir?'

Well, the baby may or may not have been in heart failure, but his mother nearly was when that possibility was voiced.

The senior doctor wheeled around to sneer at the young girl peering out from behind her colleagues.

'Does this baby *look* like he's in heart failure?' he mocked, as the student's face changed colour to a beetroot red. I have to say, the infant lying on his back, having been unceremoniously woken up, was now waving his arms and legs vigorously and wasn't exactly being helpful. Apart from his bloated appearance, he had reached the crescendo of full voice, belying the fact that there could possibly be anything feeble or oxygen-starved about his lungs or circulatory system.

The paediatrician turned back to me and told me, in a very patronising way, that, despite my child's fluid retention, I probably had an over-enthusiastic midwife, who really should not have alarmed everyone by insisting on my baby's admission to hospital. He told me I could take him home if I liked, but I should just keep an eye on him and see how he goes—as if I was going to take him home and stuff him in a cupboard and forget to look at him.

As things turned out with Philip Junior, I have always really, really wished that I knew who the medical student was, who was so scorned at the time, so I could tell her that she had been right after all, to console her for the embarrassing put-down she suffered, and encourage her.

CHAPTER 17

All of My Life

*When I had to trust total strangers with
my baby's life*

Life was normal for us for the first fifteen months of young Philip's life (who I am now going to refer to as Phil, although we didn't call him that until he was a teenager).

You see? I did say it would cause confusion.

The fluid retention gradually subsided in the few weeks following his hospital experience, he had all his regular baby check-ups, he was never ill, and he had all his immunisations without any abnormal reactions, until the day I took him to the baby clinic for one of his booster vaccinations.

The health visitor who checked him over first was very thorough, and she listened to his chest for ages. Eventually she said she just wanted the doctor to have a listen as well. The clinic was attached to our GP surgery, so it was our family doctor who gave his second opinion. They both said that they could hear a faint heart murmur and thought it best that Phil was referred to the paediatric department at the hospital. We knew he was fit and well, so we didn't worry unduly and in due course, I received an appointment to take him to the local Children's Clinic.

The Paediatric Consultant we saw was a lovely man called

Dr Campbell. The examinations he performed were quite extraordinary, especially on such a little body. As well as all the usual checks and heart auscultation, he took blood pressure readings from every limb and several areas of every limb and cross-checked them with a simultaneous pulse count from another area. Basically, he was checking whether the blood was flowing around properly and whether there were any palpable delays in rhythm or beat, or weak pulses.

I was more fascinated than worried. I really thought they were looking for something that wasn't there and, at the end of the consultation, he would tell me not to worry, everything was okay.

I could not believe what I was hearing when Dr Campbell told me that he would be referring Phil on to the Royal Liverpool Children's Hospital in Myrtle Street, which was where the regional paediatric cardiac centre was. He said that he was almost certain that Phil would need heart surgery to correct a congenital deformity in the major vessels of his heart and it would need doing without further delay.

I had to really bite my tongue to prevent myself from telling him that he was most certainly wrong and did he think I wouldn't have known if my child was seriously ill? What sort of inattentive mother did he take me for? Instead, I heard myself thanking him, and then I left the hospital, clutching Phil to me and walking to the car in a complete daze.

When Philip came home from work, I told him what had gone on and what the consultant had told me. He, too, sort of half-laughed and pulled a face of disbelief and said that surely they had got it wrong.

We were sent a letter to attend an outpatient's appointment at the RLCH, so we arranged for Esther to be looked after and David to be picked up from school, packed up some lunch, and set off for

Liverpool. Neither of us had ever been to Liverpool before, we had no road map and, of course it was in the days before satnav. There was the usual scrappy little drawing of an approximation of the area where you were supposed to end up, included in the appointment card, but it bore no resemblance to the area we ended up driving around.

We always find that these sorts of directions make no reference to the fact that you will always find yourself in a one-way system, and that particular area of the city was no exception. The annoying thing was, we could see the hospital. We could have got out of the car at more than one set of traffic lights and just hopped over the road to the building, but it took us about 40 minutes to locate anywhere to park the car and find the official entrance. Fortunately, we had allowed plenty of time to get there, but the frustration of the journey did nothing for the state of our nerves.

Myrtle Street Children's Hospital, as it was formerly known, was an ancient building that had stood on that site since 1869, with warren-like corridors, all half-illuminated by dingy, city-soiled windows. I later found out that my dad had attended the eye department for a series of treatments at the same hospital when he was a child, after someone had shot him in the eye with a toy bow and arrow! The surgeons who worked there had started performing open heart surgery on children in 1956, which had given it international fame. There was always a peculiar, gassy, sulphur-like smell, which I can still recall, that I think emanated from the miles of cast iron pipes that were attached to the ceiling of every corridor. It was a generally dark and dismal Victorian building, and the outpatients' waiting room had a similarly forbidding atmosphere.

I can't remember much about that first appointment, only that I was still convinced that they had the wrong patient notes, and they had mixed Phil up with another child who was really ill and needed life-saving surgery. I was absolutely ready for the moment when a senior member of staff would come and apologise profusely for dragging us all this way to Liverpool for nothing, but it never came. They did all the ultrasounds, echo scans, x-rays, and blood tests which were necessary, none of which impressed Phil overly much.

They used a wonderful local anaesthetic cream to numb the area on his hands and arms where they wanted to take blood from, but he didn't like that either and no amount of trying to distract his attention took his eyes away from the particular area of his anatomy they were wanting to fiddle with. Eventually, all the pre-op tests were done, and we were sent home with the instructions to bring him back the following week, when he would have a cardiac catheterisation performed under heavy sedation, followed by the heart operation a couple of days later.

I cannot describe the awful feelings and emotions that surge through your mental and physical system, knowing that your 22-month-old baby is shortly going to be subjected to major heart surgery and you are going to have to hand him over to relative strangers whom you are going to have to trust with his life. It goes against every instinct and, whilst your basic, animal, protective reflexes come rushing to the fore, some tiny seed of common sense in the back of your sub-conscious tells you to let go and do what you have been told.

Thankfully, there is also a safety valve which is triggered in these types of circumstances, which somehow numbs part of your emotions, so you don't experience the full extent of the shock and fear of the situation, so you are still able to function to some acceptable degree.

I remember bathing Phil the evening before we took him into hospital. I had taken him back to his bedroom and sat him up on his changing mat unit. I can't tell you how long I just stood looking at his perfect little chest and rib cage, with his flawless skin and grieving the fact that, in a few days' time, he would have an angry scar running horizontally from front to back around his ribs, and he would never be the same again. It is strange how the little things can upset you the most. My brain wouldn't let me focus on the seriousness of the actual operation and what was going to be physically done to his heart and surrounding major blood vessels, even though I had assisted in heart operations during my nursing days and knew exactly what it all entailed, but my main sadness was the prospect of losing his perfect skin.

We arrived back at Myrtle Street at 2:15 pm on Monday the 5th of November 1984. Every time we had visited the hospital so far, we had got lost and tied ourselves in knots trying to find the correct route because each time, we couldn't remember which road had been the wrong way or the right way, and this day was no exception. The only reason I can record, in detail, what happened during our hospital stay that year was because I recently came across an exercise book that I had filled in whilst we were there and it has a fair bit of detail written in it. I have to say, I was very surprised at the difference between then and now.

Child care and the way they were nursed in the 1980s seems to be nothing short of shocking, when you compare how modern day children's wards are run. Parents were still not overly encouraged and if you were planning on staying with your child, you had to make arrangements beforehand. You were actively discouraged from staying on the ward all day and the Ward Sister would regularly ask you to leave, so your child could get some rest or sleep. You had to ask for permission to get your child out of the cot or hold them, once preparations were underway for any procedure or operation. Reading the account I had written, it was also very clear that we just accepted that authority over us, and we would have been considered to be acting abnormally if we had questioned or rebelled against any instruction from the ward staff.

We went up to the ward, where Phil immediately made himself at home by charging up and down the ward and making a beeline for the playroom. A more robust child you could not have imagined. We felt like complete frauds and that our son was a time-waster. All the usual admission procedures were carried out and Phil was fairly compliant with most of what was happening. At one point, I left the ward briefly and when I came back in, the doctor was just finishing taking a blood test. He said they would deliberately wait until mum left the ward before they did the more distressing tests because then the child would associate mum with the comfort and consolation afterwards and not the pain of the needle.

I suppose he had a point but if they tried that sort of approach nowadays, they would be sued for assault! The doctor put a plaster over the area on his hand where the blood had been drawn from and Phil was allowed to have his tea. He tried manfully to eat, but every so often, he would look at his plaster and his bottom lip wobbled and his eyes filled with tears. We decided the best thing was to remove the plaster so it wouldn't remind him of his dreadful ordeal and once that was done, he finished his hamburger and chips in a somewhat better frame of mind.

The nurse had said that there would be a firework display at 6:00 pm in the yard outside the window, as it was bonfire night. I got Phil in his pyjamas, ready for bed, and he put the playroom through its paces again until it was time for the fireworks.

Two minutes before the first firework was lit, a nurse came to get Phil, saying he needed to go for another echo scan, but he wouldn't be long. I had to stay on the ward, so I watched the fireworks. Phil was brought back forty minutes later, sobbing his eyes out, and, to add insult to injury, he had missed the display altogether. It was such a shame, and as I write this, it upsets me to think how much these little ones had to go through on their own, because parents weren't allowed to attend certain procedures.

We had cuddles, and he calmed down after a while, so I put him down to sleep in his hospital cot, and I was told by the staff to go and get my supper in the dining room. After that I was taken to the room where I would sleep. It was a couple of floors up from Phil's ward and it was, well... basic. The room was a sort of curved shape, with windows along one wall and huge painted murals of nursery rhyme characters on all the others. There were four camp beds set up and a tiny square shelf on which perched a kettle. There was no sink to fill the kettle from and the only toilet, I was told, was on the next floor up. I subsequently learnt that the knack to filling the kettle was to sneak onto the nearest ward when Sister was otherwise occupied and fill it as quickly and quietly as the tap would allow from the ward kitchen sink. If you were caught, she would bellow and tell you to get off her ward. The supplies to make a drink with the stolen hot water were your own responsibility.

I went back onto Phil's ward and found him fast asleep on his tummy, directly on top of the plastic sheet, with his feet sticking out through the cot bars. I managed to re-arrange him without waking him up and put the sheet back under him, then I went back to my palatial quarters. The one good thing about the antiquated building was that the bath tubs were of the claw-footed, cast iron variety that I had enjoyed in the nurses' home during my training in Manchester. I had a good nosy along the corridor until I found a bathroom and I claimed it, making full use of the deep and plentiful hot water, then went back to the mothers' room and tried to get some sleep. Unsurprisingly, I did not get to sleep for hours and then I only dozed until the time came when I would be allowed back on the ward the following morning.

When I got onto the ward, Phil had already had his pre-med and the nurses had changed him into his tiny little operating gown. The ward sister told me that he would go to theatre for a cardiac catheterisation at 9:15 am. This procedure involved making a small incision in his groin and feeding a tube up and through the arteries until it reached the heart and out the other side. Radio-opaque dye is injected and the progress of the catheter can be seen on the x-ray screen, so the surgeons have a pretty good idea of the width and restrictions of the various vessels. They do this, so they can plan the surgery procedure with as much information as possible. To a cardiac surgeon, this is a routine procedure, but it wasn't quite so routine to us!

Philip was given an injection of morphine on the ward, which really upset him. By now, he was starting to cry when any of the staff approached him because, so far, most of them had stuck needles in him at some point and even the magic cream which numbed the skin wasn't fooling him. At 9:15 am precisely, Sister came to get him and took him down to the operating theatre, and I was instructed to go and get a cup of coffee. You were not allowed to stay on the ward if your child wasn't there, so I did as I was told. She said he would be back at 10:45 am and I could come back then.

When I returned, I had to wait in the dirty, smoky, waiting room until they had 'sorted him out', whatever that entailed, and they had also moved his cot nearer to the nurse's station, so they could keep a closer eye on him. It was important that he stayed asleep for at least an hour, or he would have a nasty headache, so he was still sedated. Not only that, he had to stay lying down for eight hours, otherwise the dye that was used and the fact that they had been poking about in his heart could cause problems with his blood pressure and could cause brain damage, if he didn't stay horizontal.

This was just the preliminary procedure. They hadn't done the proper heart surgery yet!

He kept waking up during the rest of the day and I kept getting sent off the ward because they considered it was upsetting for him when he wanted me to pick him up but I wasn't allowed to.

Thankfully, he was kept fairly drowsy, but keeping a toddler of that age in a prone position for many hours is quite a feat.

In the early evening, I was looking out of the window that overlooked the road outside. I noticed a policeman had arrived in his van and was putting cones out in front of the hospital to stop traffic coming past. We were all idly wondering what was happening, when a phone call came through to the ward. Apparently, there was a bomb scare in the pub across the road!

So, whilst the rest of Liverpool was being kept out of the area for their own safety, we were trapped there like sitting ducks. Not to worry, though. The health and safety measures of the day were galvanised into action. The babies were moved away from the windows and the staff drew the blinds and curtains, 'in case the windows blow in!' There were half a dozen fire engines and a good proportion of the entire city's police force gathered outside as the bomb squad prepared controlled conditions to detonate the suspicious package in, which had been found inside the pub opposite.

We were warned to prepare ourselves for the blast—how, I'm not quite sure. We waited with baited breath for what seemed like hours, but the bang never came. Maybe someone had claimed the package and explained its presence, or maybe they just thought better of it. Anyway, it was somewhat of an anti-climax, not that I particularly wanted a spectacular explosion that would endanger the lives of hundreds of sick children, you understand, but I did rather wonder what they had planned for the following evening, having laid on fireworks and anticipated bomb blasts for the two evenings we had been in residence so far.

CHAPTER 18

All I Can Do

Learning to accept what I had no control over

When I went on the ward the following morning, I could see that, although he was still lying down, Phil was awake. As I arrived at his cot side, he looked at me through glazed eyes and it took a couple of seconds to register that it was me, and then he beamed at me and wanted to be picked up. I was allowed to give him some Weetabix for breakfast, the first thing he had eaten since the Monday evening when we first arrived. He was ravenous and very thirsty all day. He was weighed later that morning and the nurse seemed surprised that he had lost weight. I was very tempted to point out the obvious, that the child had been starved for two days and there wasn't much in the way of fat reserves to begin with, but I didn't.

His Elastoplast dressing was removed from his groin later that day, and he couldn't have made more noise if the nurse had taken his leg off with it. He had developed a very good line in looking mortally wounded and perfecting his bottom lip tremble, every time he looked at the injured area. We had a minor panic when I realised at one point that the towelling nappy that was his cuddle blanket had been whisked away in the laundry skip when his bed had been made earlier. The male nurse who was on duty said not to worry, he would go and have a rummage through the dirty laundry and see if he could find it. That would definitely not happen nowadays. He came back with a triumphant look on his face, waving the errant nappy. I had already given Phil a clean one and I would wash the lost one before I allowed him to have it back, I hasten to add.

I was called down to Dr Arnold's office that afternoon, to discuss their findings from the previous day. He told me that Phil had been very co-operative and the procedure had gone very well. I supposed that he would have been very co-operative, with half a gallon of Morphine in his system, but again, I restrained myself from pointing that out.

Dr Arnold was the consultant physician and was a very friendly, reassuring chap who insisted on drawing me a detailed diagram of the operating team's intentions during the surgery which would take place the following day.

The condition Phil was born with is known as a Coarctation of the Aorta. This means that the arch of the aorta coming out of the heart had a severe restriction, and was so narrow there was hardly any blood flowing through it, despite it being the major blood vessel in the body. This was why he had no discernible pulses in his feet or his left arm and the left side of his heart had been working extremely hard to pump the blood around. The collateral, usually small, blood vessels around his heart had adapted to compensate and had developed more significantly up to this stage and were carrying the blood on a bypass route. That was what had been happening when Phil had been taken into hospital at two weeks old but the condition had not been picked up at that stage.

The reason it had not been diagnosed was because his was not a standard, text book presentation of the condition. The narrowing was in an unusual place so the operation had to be performed in a unique way. Sometimes the restricted part can be removed and the two normal width edges sutured back together, which is quite straightforward, or the artery supplying the arm can be used as a graft onto the aorta. Neither of these options were possible so the team had to discuss an alternative battle plan that had not been executed before. Dr Arnold told me that he had a wonderful lady surgeon from America on his team, called Miss McKay, who was an expert in this field and an excellent needlewoman as well.

He did explain that, because there would be very little of the normal aortic tissue left at the point of the repair, they would only be able to put a small graft in at this operation, so it would not grow with him for very long, therefore it was highly likely that he would need a second operation during childhood, and he would probably be under the cardiac team at Liverpool for the rest of his life. They had also discovered he had a deformed aortic valve, but because it seemed to be working sufficiently at that stage, they would address any problems later on, probably when he was an adult.

It is very strange, how you can hear all this completely new information, sat in a cardiac consultant's office in the basement of the best paediatric coronary care hospital in Europe, at the time, and just nod politely. The fact that all this information applied to my baby boy seemed so disconnected from our actual situation that, even now, I wonder at how anyone's brain can process such a prospect.

The fact is, it can't. That self-protecting safety valve kicked in again and I think half my brain was switched off for a while. The half still working was very hazy for several days, and I am so glad I wrote a diary at the time because I have not recalled these details in my head since that time.

Phil was due to go into theatre at 9:00 am the following day, so I knew it would be another sleepless night for me, but I was so, so grateful that Phil knew nothing of what was to come. That was the advantage of having a little one in hospital. They only got upset after a deed had been done: they didn't have the agony of the anticipation as well.

Miss McKay came to see Phil at 7:30 am, to check him over. She was a substantially built lady and looked like she would be more suited to an occupation as a vet, wrestling with large animals, rather than someone who was shortly going to be peering at my baby's tiny arteries through a microscope and suturing vessels that were barely distinguishable to the naked eye. She had a lovely, reassuring manner though and I felt completely confident that she was the best person for the job. She again explained most of what Dr Arnold had told me the day before but emphasised that they were virtually going to have to make it up as they went along, once they got in there and whatever they did would be a pioneering version of the repair.

Again, I nodded politely and thanked her.

The theatre trolley arrived at exactly the time the ward sister said it would—it was clear who was in charge in those days—and she picked up Phil's drowsy little frame and gently placed him on the trolley. Despite her brusque and authoritative exterior, it was obvious that she really cared about her small charges. The way she carefully tucked the blanket around him and kept her hand on top of him all the way out of the ward was such a loving gesture.

'Say goodbye to Mum,' she said and walked off with him. Philip arrived shortly after, and we were at a bit of a loose end until Phil came back on the ward. We weren't allowed to stay on the ward and the waiting room was quite depressing and dirty, so we decided to go outside and have a walk in the fresh air, or as fresh as you can get in Liverpool city centre in November. We soon found the Cathedral and spent some time wandering around. It is a peculiarly calming and comforting building inside and it became our 'go-to' escape on many future occasions, when Phil was having an operation or giving us cause for anxiety.

It was lunchtime before Phil was returned to the ward. I was amazed when we were allowed to see him. I had envisioned him to look dreadful and scary, but he looked perfectly okay. He had an intravenous drip and lots of attachments to monitor his vital signs, but nothing alarming at all. His head was inside a Perspex 'head box' which was supplying him with oxygen but his colour all looked normal. They only let us stay with him for a few minutes then we were told to go and get some lunch and come back later.

When we returned, he was getting very agitated and trying to pull his drip out and succeeded in pulling all his monitors off. He was very frightened and looked anxiously at us through the head box as if to say, 'For goodness sake! Are you not going to do anything about my predicament?'

He was given more Morphine to calm him down, and we went back in to see him every hour and were relieved to see that he was much calmer as time went on.

It is dreadful, not being able to pick up your baby when you know he is distressed and worse still to know that he can't understand why you are not making things better for him. I consoled myself by thinking that at least he wouldn't remember any of this and, as time went on, it would be easier to bring him into hospital for further procedures because he would be older and it wouldn't worry me so much.

How naïve I was! Of course it didn't get easier. It was just that each time was different and had its own unique set of circumstances to worry about.

Miss McKay came to see us and explained what they had found and how they had fashioned a repair. The constriction had been very tight and the aorta had been virtually closed, so she had inserted a larger patch than anticipated. This initial patch had been made from a preserved pericardium, but she said the repair would definitely have to be maintained over the next few years and replaced with a bigger one as he grew. It wasn't possible to put a large patch in to start with, as it would affect his blood pressure. It had taken a very skilful team to achieve this repair, and they had so many factors to take into consideration to give him the best quality of life. It was just so incredible that this child had such a massive deformity in his heart but had no discernible symptoms in everyday life.

I went to bed that night with such a relieved heart and secure in the knowledge that a nurse had been taken from another ward to special him throughout the night. It may be a strange concept to realise how little the mums were allowed to be involved with the care of their children in those days, but the premium quality of care from the nursing staff was absolutely guaranteed.

He was a model patient whilst he was kept sedated, apart from his blood pressure and high temperatures causing concern, but by the third day, he had had enough of lazing about. He sat up in his cot and very carefully and systematically pulled off every wire and monitor attached to him, and then completed his act of rebellion by pulling his drip out. It wasn't done in a temper: he removed each component individually, very slowly and deliberately. He had kept all the night staff entertained by singing to them most of the night, apparently, so they were delighted with him. He was allowed some breakfast and a bed bath that morning, and already started to look more like himself.

It was really difficult handling him over the next few days, as he was obviously in great pain, especially with the nappy changing, but he was gradually mobilised and got very used to the hospital way of life. On his fifth day post-op he tried a little walk but went quite wobbly, which seemed to knock his confidence a bit, and he remained very clingy for the rest of his stay, but, ten days after he was first admitted, we were allowed to take him home.

It was the most wonderful feeling. It felt like I was bringing home a new baby from hospital. I had no idea just how tense I had been in Liverpool until we had been home a few days and then the reality of all that had happened started to hit me. It took me several weeks to adjust back to the normal activities of life and emotionally process what had happened.

CHAPTER 19

Superstar

My next-door neighbour mother-figure

Phil healed so quickly and so well. It is remarkable how young children bounce back, and 'bounce' is the word. We had to physically restrain him from being too active because of the healing that was going on in his body. Toddlers don't know they are supposed to be ill, so if it doesn't hurt, it doesn't bother them.

I was so well supported by my wonderful neighbour, who took great delight in being involved in our family life as much as possible. Lilian had lost her husband to a brain tumour not long before we moved next door and it seemed to give her back a focus in life when she was able to help us.

She was of our parents' generation and very hardworking and still operating by traditional, old-fashioned methods. Her house was the same layout as ours but still had no central heating or upstairs toilet. I know her daughter will not mind me divulging the information that Lilian kept a 'gazzunder' (chamber pot) under her bed, and used it on a nightly basis.

Her daily routine was set in stone and never varied. She would get up at a ridiculously early time every morning, take her pot, and carefully carry it downstairs to the toilet just off the kitchen, empty it, clean it, and replace it under her bed. She would have her breakfast and partake in her morning ablutions, get dressed, make her bed, tidy the bedroom and get everything ready for work. She worked in the office of a feed mill just down the road and would always get a lift in to work by a fellow worker who you could set your clock by when they beeped their car horn on the road outside Lilian's house to announce their arrival.

Before she left the house, she would have emptied out the old ashes from her fireplace in her tiny living room—which were probably still warm from the night before, she got up so early— then lay the new fire, ready to light when she came back into the house later on, just after four o'clock. She would clean around everywhere, wash all her breakfast dishes and clean the kitchen and everything was like a new pin every day. Nothing was ever out of place but yet it was still homely and welcoming.

As soon as she returned home from work, she would light her fire, replace the spark guard, and come straight round to our house for a cup of tea whilst her fire got going and warmed the downstairs through. She was hilarious. She was so down to earth and motherly, it was a pleasure to live so close by and share our lives with her.

She loved ironing and would insist that I sent all my ironing round to her. In those days, most of the clothing we wore needed to be ironed if you didn't want to look like you'd just dropped off the back of something and it was a never-ending task. She would get through it all at a great rate, but her favourite items were shirts. She would iron the shirts with such precision, skill, and attention to detail, she would even button them up completely and refold them as they were when they were sold in their packets. Philip never minded this at all, but I believe it drove her son-in-law mad whenever Lilian did her daughter's ironing, because he hated the fact that he had to spend all that time unbuttoning his shirts before he could get dressed! She was undeterred though, and I'm sure she carried on folding and buttoning up her son-in-law's shirts just for badness and to annoy him.

I helped her decorate her bedroom over the space of about a week, on one occasion. We did it in stages, and she managed to shift the furniture into the middle of the room, and we worked around everything by degrees. I was standing on her stepladder one evening, painting the window frame. I must have been remarking on some bits that weren't perfect and a couple of areas that I had smudged onto the glass.

'Ah, don't worry about it,' she said. 'A man on a galloping horse isn't going to notice that!' I turned around to smile at her and found her perched on top of her old-fashioned wardrobe, swinging her little legs and wielding a paintbrush which was dripping so much that most of the paint was in her hair. She looked so comical, I nearly fell off my perch, laughing. She was very small of stature but quite round in shape and I will never forget the picture in my head of her having clambered onto the furniture to get a better reach and ending up six inches off the ceiling, trying to peer sideways through her paint-splattered glasses to see what she was doing.

I only knew Lilian for five years but in that time, she was a true mother-figure in my life. She would babysit, we would have her over for meals, we shared gardening and cooking activities and I like to think she looked on me as her second daughter. She always made me feel very special, and she loved my family like her own. She died from a sudden heart attack one day, at the age of 58 and her death hit me hard. Our kitchen windows overlooked each other across our adjoining driveways and for weeks after she died, I couldn't bear to have my kitchen window blind open because I would have to look across at her empty house. I have always felt privileged to have known Lilian and to have benefitted so much from her selfless and generous disposition. She taught me a lot about life, but I have always been sad that my children didn't get the chance to know her for a lot longer, or know her at all, in our fourth child's case.

Phil needed further maintenance procedures following his initial operation, and he went back for his first follow-up as an inpatient when he was three years old. The repair patch had been holding up well but was causing a noticeable change in his blood pressure. Dr Arnold decided to do a 'balloon catheter' procedure to stretch the patch to extend its life somewhat. It involved a general anaesthetic and inserting a catheter into the groin, as with the diagnostic procedure, but when the catheter tip reached the site of the repair, which they could see on the x-ray screen, it was blown up like a balloon within the aorta, which stretched the patch sufficiently to cope with a few years' more growth. Although it was a fairly routine procedure, it was not without its risks. If they tried to stretch the patch too much all at once, it could rupture, which of course would cause a catastrophic emergency.

We had got fairly blasé with outpatient appointments and the interim procedures which were extending the length of time before it would be necessary to perform a further major operation to replace the patch with a newer, larger one, so it became a regular occurrence in our house that Phil and I would go and stay in hospital periodically. On one such occasion, when David and Esther were being bathed by their grandma, they asked her, 'When will it be our turn to go and stay in hospital?'

Thus, our lives went on, with regular trips to the Liverpool Outpatients Department with Phil and learning how to become proficient in double-entry bookkeeping at work, either in the office above the shop, or at home, depending on the school term.

The office upstairs at Porter's was less than salubrious. It was a tiny, grubby room with two desks, shelving and a filing cabinet. There was a carpet, but whatever colour it had been originally was now heavily disguised by the traffic of various and many work boots over the years. Boots that were fresh from the most recent farm callout or delivery and were liberally coated in whatever animal residue had been left in the yard. There was usually a good selection to choose from and every excretion smelled different.

Even from the office upstairs, I could tell when a pig farmer had entered the shop on market days. Cows, hens, sheep, pigs, and horses all have their own identifiable odour and some are easier to cope with than others. There was one smell that was unmistakeable and if you saw the wagon go past, it was in everyone's best interest to run to the shop door and close it as quickly as you could. That was the knacker's wagon from the abattoir at the far end of the cattle market. The stench got up your nose and stayed there for the rest of the day. It was horrendous.

Farm smells, unfortunately, featured large in our family's life, with Philip coming home in his mucky boiler suits every day, and our house being situated between two stretches of fields. The two farmers who owned the land in front and behind the house didn't ever think to coordinate their muckspreading calendar with each other. Just as one finished, the other seemed to start, and they always waited until my clean washing was all pegged out on the line, ready to absorb the stench, just to create maximum impact. Strangely, though, our children seemed to be drawn to the different smells and loved to go on occasional visits to the farms with Philip whenever they got the chance. David took to spending as much free time as he could on the pig farm belonging to one of his uncles. He learnt everything there was to know about pigs and their piglets, and, although he would be horrified at being asked to clear the lawn of dog dirt, he took great delight in shovelling out the pig buildings every weekend. Needless to say, he was 'encouraged' to leave his aromatic boiler suit outside the back door when he came home. I could not abide the smell of pig muck.

I remember taking a visit to the abattoir on one occasion, just before Phil was due to go into hospital for another procedure. I went to see if they could let me have a fresh heart still attached to the lungs of a pig.

I thought it was a perfectly reasonable request.

As it happened, when I explained that I wanted to do my own biology lesson to show my son what was going on inside his own body, the bloke who was hosing the blood and guts off the floor also thought it was an entirely normal thing to want to do, so he told me to come back the next day, when he had made sure that a set of the required organs were removed carefully and intact. He even wrapped them up for me in greaseproof paper but told me not to keep them for long as they would start to smell very quickly.

That was obviously the problem with his wagon and the reason why it regularly shared its stink with the local residents. It was the lingering lungs.

I took my slaughterhouse-fresh organs home with great delight and slapped them on the kitchen counter. David and Esther took one horrified look, turned slightly green and disappeared out of the room faster than I could turn around. Phil, however, was fascinated, and we spent quite some time inspecting all the chambers, valves, and vessels of the heart, inspecting the relative area where he had had his surgery and sticking a straw down the trachea and blowing air through the whole arrangement to inflate the lungs. I'm not sure it's something that would be encouraged on the school syllabus nowadays, but it was very interesting, if you had the stomach for it.

Nobody was very keen on coming down for tea that evening. They clearly did not trust me enough not to cook the things and serve them up, disguised under the gravy!

CHAPTER 20

This Masquerade

The furore of getting a small child
changed into a costume

We had always planned to have four children, but in two lots of two, so they would be playmates for each other. We managed it with David and Esther, with only sixteen months between them, but Phil's health issues really threw a spanner in the works. I had also applied to be a childminder and start a business from home before we realised the implications of our regular hospital visits and inpatient stays, so that idea was shelved as well. The consultant at Liverpool had advised us against having another child because there would be a very high statistical chance of another baby being born with congenital heart problems, but the idea kept nagging at me.

My mind was made up one day, when I was getting everyone ready to leave the house and the three children trooped down the hallway and through the doorway to the living room. I realised I had mentally counted them through, but then found myself looking down the hall for the fourth one. It was a bizarre moment, but we decided that it was a sign that we should complete our family with another baby, and we would take the chance of a statistical health risk. After all, David and Esther were completely okay and healthy. It was also statistically proven at the time that one in every four babies in the world was Chinese, so I suppose we had to take that risk on board as well.

I'll not trouble you with the details—nobody is that desperate for a bit of spice in their lives—but suffice to say, we were fortunate to be able to conceive babies more or less when we wanted them. At the time, we did not realise how much of a blessing that was, but we were still very excited then, when we realised in the latter half of 1987, that number four was on the way.

It was quite comical noting people's reactions when we told them we were expecting again. The looks usually involved a raised eyebrow and a tentative, 'Oh, really? And are you pleased?' sort of enquiry, just to confirm what the correct reaction should be, in case we hadn't planned this one.

My dad did suggest that we find out what was causing all these babies, but I knew he was delighted.

Phil had just started school that September, though he was only going for half days until Christmas because the staff were very wary of his condition and didn't want to be responsible for him getting overtired, so they encouraged us to let him adjust gradually. That meant four trips a day down to the village school, which wouldn't have been too bad normally as it was only a few hundred yards down the road, but fitting in four walks a day around the nausea and vomiting of my pregnancy was a bit of a challenge.

Modern mums think they invented the much-debated practice of doing the school run in their pyjamas, but I can tell you, they didn't: I did.

I would haul my nauseous self out of bed that autumn term and hold my breath whilst I made two lots of sandwiches, trying desperately not to inhale the smell of the food cupboard. David and Esther got themselves ready for school whilst I attempted to put a new school uniform onto Phil with one hand, whilst operating the toilet flush handle with the other.

I had had a brainwave that summer and decided that I had had enough of tying school ties every day, so when I bought the third Woodplumpton School tie, I decided to doctor it. I knotted it in the normal way around a child's neck—whichever child was the most co-operative at the time—and loosened it off to leave an extra length of fabric around the back of the neck. I cut the tie at the back of the neck, sewed Velcro (other hook and eye tapes are available) onto each cut end, then sewed the knot in place at the front so that the tie knot stayed fastened—that detail is very important. Each morning or after PE at school, the child could just place the tie around his/her neck and close the Velcro, instead of tying the thing from scratch.

I didn't actually patent my design, although I should have done, as it impressed the school staff and the head teacher was soon making recommendations that other parents of new children should do the same with their ties. It saved hours in the classroom. Most primary schools have retired the old school tie in favour of a polo shirt nowadays, but if that little tip is something that will make your life easier, feel free to use the idea.

So, when I had three children who looked something like decent, I would pull some loose trousers and a sloppy jumper on over my nightie, my big coat over the top and walk down the road to drop them at the school gate. After the obligatory cheery greetings to other mums, I would totter back home, grab a cup of tea and go back to bed, hoping the tea would stay down for long enough to settle things in the vomiting department, then make sure I was up again in time to walk up to school and collect Phil at lunchtime. I did get dressed properly then. Even I couldn't justify still having my nightie on at lunch time. Phil and I would trot down the road again at 3:30 to pick David and Esther up and pretend we had spent the afternoon productively, when in fact, he'd had a nap after lunch and I had watched some trite drama on the telly, whilst mentally reprimanding myself that I really should be hoovering. The problem with this type of self-disciplinary thought process is that you absolutely agree with every word emanating from the voice inside your head—yet you continue to sit, watching the telly.

I was always very grateful that all my children, up to that point, had loved starting school. They had all trotted in on their first day with anticipation and excitement and had settled down really well. Of course, it may well have had a lot to do with the reception class teacher at the time, Mrs Waite, who was very good at her vocation. She was the epitome of the first teacher you would want your child to experience and I'm sure that moulded my kids' attitude to school life forever after. She was firm but kind and understanding. No child got away with anything they shouldn't, but she was a lot of fun and the children really responded to her teaching methods and thought the world of her. She taught her charges to be respectful of their elders and considerate of others.

I'm sure she wondered what she was taking on when David started though. He was a very mild mannered child but if he got wound up, he would react. His cousin was in the same class and one day, fairly early in David's school career, they had a falling-out. It wasn't the first falling-out they had experienced and in the past, David had always been the one to come off worse. Now I couldn't possibly say who the instigator was on this occasion and there was a fair bit of shoving and pushing involved, but suffice to say, David ended up banging his cousin's head against the wall in the playground. There was blood. There was also a trip to A & E which involved some suturing, but thankfully, the young cousin's parents were of an understanding nature, and we all agreed it was probably six of one and half a dozen of the other.

Esther's infant school career was not without its moments either. She was a little dot. Slight of build and very shy, the teachers probably did not think she was capable of asserting herself. As long as she had a book to read and a corner to retreat to, she was no trouble. She was the youngest girl in her year, so in the summer of 1984, she was chosen to present a bouquet of flowers to the Lady Mayoress at the opening of the annual church garden party which was held in the school grounds that year. Each class in the school had prepared a piece to perform for the parents and visitors and the reception class had been practising for a teddy bears' picnic. All the costumes had been successfully tried on at home, and they all knew the songs, so everyone was set to go.

What we hadn't taken into consideration was Esther's complete phobia of taking her clothes off in public. Now, you will be forgiven for thinking that this is normally an excellent predisposition for anybody's daughter to have and would come in very handy during her teenage years and beyond, and should be actively encouraged.

However, Esther arrived at the garden party all dressed up in a beautiful, ex-bridesmaid dress, hair up, and flower bedecked, ready to play the part of the little cherub giving the flowers to the lady of honour. The opening ceremony was completed, the photos captured of a rosy-cheeked, beaming infant child being embraced by the smiling lady in the big hat and the chain around her shoulders, and then it was time for Esther to be whisked off by a member of staff to Mrs Waite's classroom, to get her ready for her next big moment.

The big moment came a lot sooner than anyone was prepared for. I was outside amongst the stalls and activities that were laid on, when I heard a siren-type noise that started from nothing and got louder and louder. People started looking around, trying to discern what it was and where it was coming from. I had a sudden sick feeling of recognition, and I was already heading towards the infant's classroom just as a rather harassed member of staff was coming out to get me. I entered the room from the outside door, to witness a sort of minor rugby scrum. I could have sworn my daughter had the requisite number of limbs when she left home, but there seemed to be rather more than two arms and two legs being kicked out and flung around from underneath the two frazzled bodies of Mrs Waite and her classroom assistant. The two adults came up for air when they spied me, both wearing expressions of shock and disbelief.

All they had done was casually start to remove Esther's pretty dress—remember, these were the days when common sense ruled the world and adults in authority were expected to help children with such things as dressing and other personal undertakings, in order to get things done in a timely manner—and help her on with the somewhat snug-fitting teddy bear outfit, such as all her classmates were already dressed in. They had no idea that the little cherub, last seen beaming in the arms of the Lady Mayoress, was even capable of transforming into the roaring creature that was putting both sets of adult shins in grave danger. She could have been auditioning for the Incredible Hulk, only she hadn't turned green but an intense shade of puce red. The birthmarks on her eyelids and the back of her neck were showing purple and as she stood there in her vest and knickers with fists clenched and eyes flashing, she was ready to take on the world, such was her fury.

I did what any kind, gentle, understanding mother would have done on witnessing such distress in her beloved little girl. I quickly grabbed her in a half-nelson death grip, sat down on a chair to limit the area she could lash out in, although the tiny, infant classroom chairs somewhat cramped my style, pinned her arms down by her side and hung on, whilst the classroom assistant braved the manically twitching feet to feed the teddy bear suit on from the bottom up. By the time the brown velour fabric had reached her chest, Esther had stopped screaming, the sobbing was subsiding and normality was returning. With her furry hood pulled up over her fancy hairdo and cute, teddy bear ears sticking up each side of her head, she smiled a little sheepishly at us all, as if to say, 'There now. That wasn't so bad, was it?'

I escorted her back out into the sunshine and headed for the nearest cake stall. By the time the Teddy Bears' Picnic was being performed, her birthmarks had returned to almost invisibility and her tears had just about dried up. I think it took somewhat longer for Mrs Waite and her helper to process what had just happened and return to normal. They suffered the after-effects of shock for quite some time.

Esther having a meltdown was never to be witnessed again at school, presumably because no one ever risked trying to take her clothes off a second time. As parents, we headed towards her teenage years confident in the knowledge that, if anybody tried to take advantage of her, they would certainly get more than they bargained for and, what is more, the whole neighbourhood's attention would be alerted.

The siren sound was exercised on another occasion, however. She would probably have been around six or seven years of age and, whilst helping David dismantle his fleet of toy vehicles, or maybe doing it to annoy him, she inserted a toy car headlight up her nose. She was normally a very sensible, level headed child so it was somewhat of a surprise when she confessed what she had done, later in the day. I got a torch out of the junk drawer, found some new batteries, then tipped her head back and shone the light up her tiny nose. She hadn't inherited the substantial nasal proportions that some of the rest of us had, so it was quite difficult seeing what was up there, and she was not being terribly co-operative.

I decided that a trip to A & E would be in order, so we traipsed off that evening to get the benefit of someone else's torch and, hopefully, a pair of long nasal forceps. After shining his light up her nose and having a tentative exploratory poke around— rather him than me—the junior doctor in the casualty department announced that the offending object would have to be removed under anaesthetic the following day. I was thrilled. As if I hadn't spent enough time in the Children's Ward at hospital already, we were going to get another unscheduled visit.

In those days, everything was done quickly and with the minimum of waiting around. I presented her to the children's ward staff the following day, who assured me that the whole procedure would not take long.

I got her changed into a theatre gown, behind the curtains, in her own little space with nobody else looking on, so there were no dramas, and she was taken down to the operating theatre by the nurse. I was allowed to stay on the ward as they said she wouldn't be long and sure enough, half an hour later, I heard a wailing sound advancing from down the corridor. The noise gathered strength and volume as it got nearer and nearer, until the prone form of my second-born arrived on a trolley being driven by a flustered-look-ing young porter. He was a touch disconcerted by the racket and couldn't discharge his duties quickly enough and bundled her onto the bed with scant ceremony, then turned around rapidly to trundle his trolley back where it came from.

The kind, caring side of my nature is always at its best in these types of situations and I quickly ordered her to shut up, open her eyes and stop making that awful row! It took her quite a few minutes to finally open her eyes and look around and establish that she was back in real life, rather than her lightly anaesthetised dream world. It had only been a whiff of anaesthetic, so she was awake enough to get dressed and go home within a couple of hours. The nurse presented her with the car headlight in a screw-topped sample bottle and told her sternly never to do such a thing again.

Esther swore blind, and still does to this day, that she never went to sleep. She had no explanation, however, as to how the foreign object, which she admitted to inserting up her nose, was removed and was now in the glass jar as evidence.

Actually, now that I am thinking about it, I think Esther went through all her troublesome stage between the ages of five to seven years, because she did not cause us any worry later on.

She and David had been messing about on the top bunk of their bunk beds one Boxing Day evening when she was about five years old. They had got over-excited with the festivities and were very giddy. I had dished out the usual threats of what would happen if they didn't settle down and get into bed, including the 'If you fall and break your leg, don't come running to me,' classic phrase, a few minutes before there was a loud thud as a small body hit the floor from a great height.

I ran upstairs to deliver my 'I told you this would happen,' speech and picked Esther up off the floor and put her in her own bed on the bottom bunk. Half an hour later, I could still hear real sobs coming from upstairs, so I went up to do some further investigations. In my defence as a mother, David and Esther were absolute professionals in the Messing About At Bedtime Until Mum Has Been Pushed Beyond Her Limit scenario and many was the occasion when David would be extracted from the bunk bed shenanigans and made to stand at the top of the stairs until Esther had given in and gone to sleep. In this instance, I thought it was more of the same, until I found Esther in her own bed, cradling her wrist, which, on closer inspection, was an entirely different shape than it normally was, due to the egg-shaped swelling that had developed on her arm.

Boxing Day midnight found us waiting in A & E, with all the other revellers who had overdone the festive excitement, although their symptoms were, by and large, different to ours, until we were seen by the medics. The little arm was definitely broken, and she was treated to a trip to the plaster room to have a cast fitted. Her little limb, which was always stick-thin, now weighed twice as much as it did before.

There is the belief that, for every negative event there is a positive effect. Well, we had one. She had always sucked her index finger since being a baby, and the action as she was growing bigger had started to have a real impression on the shape of her top gum, which had started to curve upwards, making her teeth uneven. Now, the poor little tot hadn't got the strength to lift her hand up to her mouth with the added weight of the plaster cast on her arm, so the habit was broken and her teeth and gum got the chance to resume their natural shape.

We threatened both our subsequent children as they approached school age, that if they didn't stop sucking their fingers, we would break their arm. It worked a treat. Tough love.

CHAPTER 21

Want You Back In My Life

*Retrieving towelling nappies from the
toilet waste pipe*

Naomi Ruth was the only one of my babies not to be born at Preston Royal Infirmary. She was born in the Sharoe Green Midwifery Department, where both Philip and I were born, although it had been greatly modernised since the 1950s.

I had shuffled and limped my way through my final pregnancy, due to the advanced measure of SPD (Symphysis Pubis Dysfunction) I was suffering from. It was all I could do to occasionally waddle down the road to school and back again, then carefully lower my greatly enlarged body onto the sofa and stay there until anything occurred when I was needed urgently. David and Esther were of an age when they could be relied on to walk the short distance down the road to where the lollipop lady stood, to get themselves and Phil to school, so most days I just did the minimum and got to know the new TV soap, Neighbours, very well.

I had really struggled with this affliction, so by the time I was well overdue from my expected delivery date, I was very glad to be admitted to the antenatal ward for some bedrest. I went through the usual delays when the promise of an imminent induction day came and went, but at last, late one afternoon, a young medical student came to do the deed.

He stood by the window next to my bed for a while because he had seen a magpie outside in the trees, and he was desperately trying to find a couple more. He was singing the song...

One for sorrow, two for joy,
Three for a girl and four for a boy, etc., etc.

...and, having only seen one, he couldn't very well leave me hanging and felt duty bound to create a more positive environment. Thankfully, he found a whole family of magpies, so he felt it was okay to stop that game and move on.

As per usual, when I went into labour, things took forever initially because my kids were never in a rush to shift from a comfy position, before or after birth. Having started contractions the evening before, I spent all night heaving and sighing, probably keeping everyone else awake, and was still intact at breakfast time the following day.

Let's just say, for the sake of the fainthearted amongst you, that the ward sister took matters into her own hands and used her years of knowledge and expertise to hurry things along and my labour started to gather pace. As progress was made, I was taken into the delivery room and I spied the little Perspex baby cot out of the corner of my eye. I suddenly became completely anxious and I couldn't bring myself to look at it, out of fear. It was as if I was having my first baby, not my fourth. I went into the second stage of labour with a very different attitude than I had had with the others, and I was on a mission to evict number four as quickly as possible. I have no idea why I was so scared, it was bizarre.

As it was, I gave birth to her without incident and without pain relief, on the 8th of April 1988, and she was the biggest baby of them all at 8lb 9oz. Right there and then, my broodiness was sated. I had always wondered whether I would ever feel like I had produced my quota, or whether I would always want more. I had known women who always wished they had had more babies and I didn't think I wanted to go through the rest of my life always feeling incomplete. The question was answered right there and ever since, I knew our family was complete, and we couldn't have ordered them better.

Two boys and two girls. We were very thankful.

The novel thing about having Naomi as a baby was that the world had changed considerably since my last postnatal state in 1983. Disposable nappies were a thing. More often than not, they worked, unless you bought the cheap brands, and it revolutionised my life.

My large, yellow, nappy-soaking bucket with the black lid was given an upgrade to become the ironing bucket. It still meant that it was never empty, but its contents were now dry and clean instead of being wet and smelly.

Gone were the days when Philip and I would have to participate in the new sport of 'Nappy Grabbing' we had invented since we had become parents.

The fast-paced sporting event would be triggered quite regularly by me having the bright idea of rinsing particularly poopy towelling nappies in the toilet. The correct method of doing this was to empty out the worst and most solid elements encased in the disposable nappy liner and fabric into the toilet. So far, so good.

The next, fairly crucial, skill was to hold on to the nappy, *very firmly*, whilst flushing the toilet, in order to give the nappy a good rinse in clean (ish) water, thereby removing as much residue as possible before putting the nappy to soak in the sanitising solution bucket. Frequently, I got distracted or for some other reason, I would relinquish my hold on the nappy at completely the wrong moment and watch in dismay as the final corner of the fabric disappeared from sight around the U-bend. I had learnt, very soon after developing this rather strange habit, that if I yelled loudly enough to my husband, who in those days, used to actually respond fairly briskly to my random shrieks, he would just have time to dash out of the back door, lift the lid on the sewer inspection tank in the driveway and grab the nappy as it flashed before his eyes on its express route to join the labyrinths of Preston Town Council's sewerage system.

We developed such a knack for this pastime, that we even lodged an old walking stick in the hedge, close to the inspection lid on the drive, so it was on hand to be grabbed instantly and Philip could plunge this into the nappy from a standing position, thereby stemming its flow, instead of having to grovel on his knees, which added vital milliseconds to his personal best timings. We very rarely lost one, although, of course, the rescued nappy did need a touch more loving care and extra doses of Napisan before it could be considered fit to re-use. Our game lent a whole new concept to the fairground attraction of 'Bat the Rat'.

Because of the advent of reliable disposable nappies, all my existing terry nappies were downgraded to floor cloths—waste not, want not—and I gained at least two days a week from previous baby days when I didn't have to put the washer on a hot wash and have damp towelling displays all over the downstairs rooms.

What is more, we bought a microwave. These appliances had been popular for a while, but we were a little slow to join the trend. It meant that my fourth child didn't have to live on scrambled eggs when she started eating solid food. I could prepare and cook small amounts of real food almost instantly and, with the assistance of my Mouligrater, I could create baby mush at the turn of a wheel. I was easily pleased.

Following one of Phil's outpatient appointments at the Royal Liverpool Children's Hospital, he was again admitted for a balloon catheter procedure. This time, my parent accommodation provision had been upgraded to a room of my own. The only problem was that it was out of the main building and over the road. I had to go out of the back of the hospital, cross a very badly lit area of street, which had some very dodgy-looking characters lurking around, go through a gate into a yard where all the bins were kept and make my way up the iron fire escape. When I got through the door, I still didn't feel particularly safe because I was right at the end of what seemed to be a deserted corridor, so if anyone had followed me in, nobody would hear my cries for help!

It brought to mind a friend of ours, whose wife had once complained to him that she had been left to walk home on her own because he had gone on ahead.

'What if someone had attacked me down that dark street?' she demanded of him, looking for some apologetic, or at least sympathetic response.

'Eeh, lass, tha' needn't 'ave worried about that. As soon as he'd got you under a street lamp and seen what he'd grabbed 'old of, he'd 'ave let go quick!' came his retort.

So I consoled myself that there was electric light in the corridor, at least.

Phil had his procedure the next day, with the usual explanations of the risks involved before I signed the consent form, as I had gone through several times before with the theatre staff. This procedure had been done late on in the afternoon and when Phil came back onto the ward in the evening, I was told that the stretch had been performed okay but, it was getting near the time when we would be looking towards another full repair. He was still very sedated after the anaesthetic, but he was moaning a lot, something he hadn't done before, post-op. The nurses told me that he was fine and that I should go and get some sleep and come back in the morning.

I scuttled nervously over the road, past the bins and undesirables and breathed a sigh of relief when I reached my room. I got ready for bed whilst telling myself that Phil would be fine. He would do what he usually did after these procedures. He would lie there looking deathly pale and giving a good impression of being dangerously ill when I left the ward in the evening and be sat up in bed the following morning, rosy-cheeked and eating Rice Krispies.

I must have been asleep a couple of hours when I was woken up by the ringing of a telephone. I had no idea where this phone was but it was keeping me awake, so I got up and looked out into the corridor. There was an ancient telephone attached to the wall outside my room, so I answered it, with not a lot of patience, it has to be said. It was the night nurse on Phil's ward. She told me to come back over immediately as he had taken a turn for the worse, and he was very ill.

I got dressed as quickly as I could and ran back to the hospital, not noticing the horizontal forms lying near the bins on this occasion, and got up to the ward just as the porter had arrived to wheel Phil's bed to the intensive care unit. A couple of nurses went in with him and I had to wait outside until they had got him hooked up to all the necessary machines.

It was the middle of the night, I had no idea what was going on, I was in Liverpool, hovering outside an unfamiliar set of doors with No Admittance stamped in large letters and my son was in there fighting for his life. They didn't rush anybody into intensive care for no good reason.

After what seemed an age, the nurse came out and took me inside. They didn't know what was going on. His 15-minute observations had become abnormal, he had a temperature, his blood pressure was all over the place, he was obviously in great pain, and he was in serious trouble.

Even in that situation, the ridiculous trivia of life's habits are foremost in the mind and, because, in my mind, it was way too early to phone Philip because I would disturb his sleep and there was no point in both of us being awake, I waited until about 6:00 am before I phoned him to tell him what had happened, as far as I knew at that stage. I think it is a reaction to shock that makes you do that sort of thing. If it had been a different situation, I would have rung him straightaway, but my psyche was telling me that if I behaved normally, then these circumstances would remain normal.

The next several hours revealed that Phil was bleeding internally but it couldn't be established exactly where from. There were all manner of machines and pieces of equipment brought to his bedside to x-ray and scan him but it was several days before it could be determined where he was bleeding from. He was too unstable to be taken to the new MRI scanning equipment initially and there was much talk about taking him back to theatre, but they had to find the source of the problem first. He was kept sedated and hydrated and seemed to stabilise after a few days but it was five days later when it was decided that the emergency had calmed down and the bleeding was stopping on its own.

Thankfully, the details of those five or six days are very sketchy in my mind and Phil doesn't remember much of it. I recall it was about a week later and Phil still hadn't been allowed to eat anything, when a student radiographer came onto the unit. She told me that they were going to do a very specific type of x-ray, and she instructed me to give Phil two full glasses of a barium-based drink, so that the details of his intestines would show up better when being examined radiologically. I told her that he had not eaten for more than a week and that his system could not physically cope with that volume of liquid yet.

She insisted that he drank it and stood over us whilst he did his best to drink the foul-tasting, thick liquid. He did remarkably well, and I was astonished at just how much he was managing to swallow, when nature kicked in. Predictably, it all came back, all over the floor, narrowly missing her shoes. Although I didn't want to jeopardise the x-ray test they wanted to do, I had a certain sense of satisfaction that common sense had prevailed and, although it would have been ideal for him to have consumed a good amount of the barium drink, the radiographer should have been sensitive to the circumstances and had a more reasonable approach, instead of putting a seriously ill child through quite a distressing experience. I hope that there was a lesson learnt about assessing a situation realistically, rather than just blindly following the rule book, regardless of individual capabilities.

I was so proud of my boy, though. He went through so much during his time on the intensive care unit and hardly complained at all. He still had his scan, and they managed to confirm what they suspected the problem had been. When they had made an incision to insert the catheter into his artery the week previously, one of the instruments had gone through the artery and out the other side and perforated his bowel. It had already been mentioned that there had been a problem with the insertion in one groin, so they had aborted that attempt and used the other side instead.

I was treated with kid gloves for the rest of our stay and the staff were very careful what details they admitted to as they fully expected that we would sue the hospital, but we were just so relieved that Phil was okay, and they really had looked after him so well as soon as they realised he was dangerously ill. There was an internal inquiry, which, I'm sure, will have raised issues and established further safeguards for subsequent procedures.

CHAPTER 22

Rainy Days and Mondays

*The trauma and upheaval of building a
house extension*

Having a fourth child had made us realise that our semi-detached home was getting more than a little cramped. Although it had been marketed as a three bedroomed house when we bought it, the third bedroom was tiny and barely large enough for a single bed. Now that we knew children grew up and took up a lot of space, we were doubting the wisdom of cramming the three bigger ones permanently into one bedroom, when Naomi moved into a cot in the little bedroom.

Our reluctance to herd the older ones into the one space stemmed from the fact that David and Phil could barely look at each other without a major conflict breaking out. In the days before people carriers were invented, we were fortunate to find a Ford Granada hatchback which was the widest car available at the time, and we had an extra set of seatbelts fitted. Thus, we could fit all four children in and strap them down. However, just sitting on the same back seat in the car always created a battle ground whenever we went on a journey.

'Mum, he's looking at me.'

'Phil, stop looking at your brother.'

'But Muuum, *he's* looking at *me*.'

'Well, look somewhere else. Look out of the window.'

'I can't. He says that's his window and I can't look through it.'

'Look through the other window, then.'

'I can't. Esther's reading a book and her head's in the way.'

'Esther, stop reading your book, you know it makes you car sick.'

'No, it's fine. I'm alright. I'm not going to be sic— eeurghhh.'

'Muuuummm!!! She's thrown up all over my leg! Euwwww!'

The car would be stopped. I would rummage around for the towels and udder wipes—yes, udder wipes. The forerunner of baby wipes. We sold them for the farmers to use in the milking parlour to clean the cows' udders. I really, *really* wished Esther wouldn't always manage to project some vomit down the centre console between the front seats. You could never get it all out, and we had to live with the smell for the rest of the holidays.

I would get everyone wiped down, settled down, drinks distributed, book confiscated, children re-inserted onto back seat, sat on towels if necessary, and we would set off again.

Everything would be quiet for a while but before we had gone much further however, I would hear:

'Mum, he's looking at me...'

It was not unknown for David to walk into the bedroom he shared with Phil and bop him hard on the head if he was fast asleep but breathing heavily, and he was (and still is) incapable of walking past him without making some physical contact of some description. Given that Phil weighed only three stone, wringing wet, for most of his childhood, he carried the majority of the bruises, but still, for some inexplicable reason, could never resist back-chatting and winding his big brother up, regardless of the consequences.

Esther would attempt to distance herself from all this friction by taking all my carefully folded and stacked towels and bedding out of the airing cupboard and climbing inside to read a book in the cosy warmth and shutting the door, leaving them to get on with it. However, I didn't really think that was a suitable, long-term solution to the fair distribution of available bedroom space, and Esther had to emerge at regular intervals for feeding and suchlike, so we decided we needed an extension building on the back of our house.

We must have had a very short attention span between us, or we were living in denial, but just as we had got the inside of our house fit to live in and warm and draught-free, we made plans to pitch our living arrangements once more into muck and mess for the foreseeable future. Late that summer saw us knee deep in mud, concrete, bricks, and wet mortar—again! The footings for our new extension grew ever deeper as we failed to find solid clay, only more and more soil that would not support a two storey building that was half as big again as the original house.

The land our house was built on had been fields with numerous pits in, before it had been commandeered for housing after the first world war, so it was very much pot luck as to which bit was solid and which had been filled in to create a flat landscape.

Eventually, we had a concreted foundation and the construction, rather than destruction, work began in earnest. It wasn't too bad at first because all the work went on outside our existing living space, although the privacy issue was constantly challenged and, of course, all the dirt from outside was continually being tramped into the house. By autumn, I had made the executive decision that housework was very overrated and I awarded myself a sabbatical until the end of the year.

The one thing that couldn't be avoided, though, was the laundry.

A family of six people still generated vast amounts of dirty washing, whatever the living arrangements, but I had nowhere to dry the washing after it had been washed. Once again, I was bailed out by my neighbour (a different neighbour this time, but possibly the same washing line) and she came to the rescue and offered the use of her washing line.

If I was busy by the end of the afternoon, I would requisition daughter number one to take the plastic washing basket round next door and bring the dry clothes back home, figuring that there was little point in producing your own workforce if you didn't get the full benefit from having them. There was often a slight logistical issue, in that there would probably be more than one load of washing drying on the line, which, of course meant that the basket would not be big enough to hold all the clothes.

Being nine years old, resourceful, slightly bossy and, dare I say it, not given to over-exertion, Esther would drag her five-year-old brother round as well, despite his protestations, and make him stand with her whilst she dragged the washing off the line in any way that suited her mood. Sometimes, she didn't bother to remove the pegs, but just yanked the garment sharply downwards. It usually had the desired effect but it did nothing for my clothes peg supply, which dwindled dramatically as bits of wood and spring were catapulted at speed into distant shrubbery and over field hedges, never to be seen again.

Phil's education was being supplemented by these household management sessions and Esther also taught him how to fit the maximum amount of clean, fresh laundry into the smallest space by lifting him into the three-quarters full washing basket, complete with shoes, and encouraging him to jump up and down on it with gusto until each item was suitably squashed and compliant. She could then add more clean laundry to the basket and save another trip round next door.

My lovely neighbour used to watch their antics from her upstairs window, with camera to the fore, and fall about laughing at their impromptu entertainment package.

I tried as hard as I could to be optimistic throughout the extension build, but no amount of positive thinking was enough to get me through the final month of the extension being built, without mentally falling apart. Once the back walls of the existing house had been knocked through and the plaster dust had found its way into every crevice of the house, not to mention my person, the constant noise, mess and upheaval rendered me down into a twitching, weeping, emotional wreck. I used to sit on the stairs, clutching my baby, and cry. It was the only area where I could get some privacy. I could not wait until the day I could close the door on building materials and have my living space back.

By the end of the year, we finally had our newly extended living space back to ourselves, albeit distinctly damp-smelling from all the drying plaster, but at least we were on the right side of it all. We now had two more bedrooms, an extended dining room, a utility room and a downstairs loo, which proved to be invaluable.

The only downside, once we had got ourselves organised, was that there was now no door between the kitchen and the living room but rather, a large archway, which was too big for a standard baby gate to be of any use. I was not a fan of tripping over numerous children who were underfoot whilst I was cooking, and my dad saw that as a challenge.

He arrived at our house one day, with a pair of bespoke saloon doors, which he had painstakingly created from two lengths of louvered wood panels. They were perfect. They were about chest high to an adult so a five-year-old would have trouble scaling the height, and hung about eight inches off the floor, so a toddler couldn't squeeze underneath. They swung just like traditional saloon doors and could be secured closed with a hook on the kitchen side. I was so pleased, because I liked to know my kids were safe whilst herded and penned in the other room, when I was otherwise occupied. If Esther and Phil were messing about, and she just happened to push him through the glass door of the living room or David was hopping about because he needed the toilet and fell into the glass section of the stove door, at least they weren't burning their fingers on something hot in my kitchen.

Those kids never thought about just how expensive it was to replace doors and stove glass strips.

It was lovely to be able to spread out a bit in our living space now we had our full complement of children. Naomi was a delightful baby. I had the advantage of having the experience of three previous babies, combined with the novelty of having a single baby without other toddlers to referee and forestall, because of the age difference between her and Phil. David and Esther were aged ten and nine, and they were very helpful and quite besotted with their new sister. Compared with the skinny little babies I had produced previously, Naomi was quite a sturdy little thing. As a toddler, she had thighs to be proud of and could actually wear skirts that stayed up, rather than having to wear pinafores or trousers held up with braces, like her siblings. The others took delight in nicknaming her 'Knomi' and there are several photos of her being trundled around the garden in a wheel barrow.

One of her favourite things to do, even before she could walk, was to stand up to a coffee table we had in the living room, where a small keyboard used to live. This keyboard had a demo button and, when pressed, it would play a tune, ad infinitum, demonstrating all the rhythms and sounds it was capable of. The constant sound of this thing could drive any previously sane person to the point of insanity, but Naomi loved it and would hold on to the low table and rock from side to side, in perfect rhythm with the music for hours. We have various videos of her, dressed just in a nappy, hefty little bottom swinging to the beat and hair awry, performing her own dance routines with the occasional bending of the knees for variety, but essentially repeating the same movements over and over.

She was always smiling and had the most impressive mop of curls, which she did not like being combed, and which her father always referred to as 'an explosion in a mattress factory'. It is quite ironic that she was the chunkiest of my children, because as she grew up, she became even more slender than the rest of her lean siblings. She still has the curls if she can be persuaded to stay away from the hair straighteners. She got away with a lot more than the others did, partly because of her cheeky charm and partly because her brothers and sister indulged her like they were never indulged. I don't think she and Esther ever fell out and if her brothers wound her up, she could hold her own, and they usually came off worse.

She and Phil got into an affray one day which resulted in Phil being on the receiving end of a green felt tip pen which, for whatever reason, Naomi had thrust in his direction, and it ended up in his eye. Phil was frequently the victim of random actions by other family members, though not always the innocent party, it has to be said.

We saw the inside of the A & E department at Preston more than a couple of times, like the time he got in the way when David was pretending to train for Wimbledon with his tennis racquet, using a piece of coal, substituted for a ball. Turned out, David was an excellent shot and executed a perfect lob, directing the piece of coal right into Phil's mouth. Phil managed to retain all his teeth, but the coal made a bit of a black, bloodied mess for a while. Despite him having a hospital file thick enough to use as a booster seat, Phil was never ill, unless there was a third person involved to provoke a medical incident, but we certainly got our money's worth out of the NHS with him.

He was a high-maintenance child and not just medically speaking.

He had a penchant for wandering off and getting lost when we were away from home. Many a time we would be on holiday, walking around a completely unfamiliar city or town centre with four children in tow, when we would realise we were down to three. Phil would be missing. He would be nowhere in sight and, although it wasn't the first occurrence of such a happening, the panic would start to build in me during the first few seconds of realisation.

We eventually got into the habit of scanning the unfamiliar rows of shops until we found the music shop, and head for that direction as rapidly as we could, without losing any more children in the process.

There would always be a music shop, and he would always be inside, nonchalantly wandering around the array of instruments on display, completely oblivious to the fright he had engendered in his family—well, in his mother, anyway. His siblings weren't particularly bothered.

There was one occasion when Phil had been allowed to go on a youth holiday. It was a week-long, church-based camping holiday, the first time he had ever been away without us and where somebody else would take full responsibility for him. Our slight sense of trepidation was not without justification.

Apparently, after an action-packed afternoon of entertainment at a nearby Butlin's resort, the kids had all piled on the bus which was to take them back to their own camp, in time for their evening meal. It was some time later, a good hour or more, in fact, when one of the leaders realised that he could not see Phil in the marquee where everyone was gathered. After asking around and conducting a preliminary search, it was decided that the only action left was for an adult to go back to the Butlin's park, where Phil had last been seen.

Sure enough, as the leader's car approached the entrance to the resort, there was Phil, sitting on the wall, where he had been for the last two hours, waiting quite calmly for someone to come and get him. Thankfully, due to his wanderlust, we had always impressed on him to stay put if ever he got lost and not to roam about. So that's what he did. He would still have been there at breakfast time if he had not been missed at supper!

The only place he did not stand still and wait was when he got lost quite regularly in our local Asda store. He had sussed out the Customer Service desk from a very young age and if I was out of sight at any point during the weekly shopping trips because he had got distracted and lagged behind, he would make his way to the desk. The staff there would make a fuss of him and give him sweets. He was not daft! Phil was never worried because he always reckoned that he wasn't lost. He knew exactly where he was and it was me who was lost.

There was a period in my life when I rarely went into Asda without an announcement coming over the tannoy at some point stating, 'We have a little boy in our store who is lost. His name is Philip Parkinson. Would the parent or guardian please come to the Customer Service desk to collect him?' I got to the stage where, if I was more than two-thirds through my shopping list, I would finish off my shopping and collect him from the desk on my way out of the store. It was a very cheap and efficient child care arrangement.

We always had a household of pets as well as children. After the demise of Mandy, our original cocker spaniel, we had brought home a Border Collie pup, much to our children's delight. There was quite a bit of discussion about what we should call her. There had been a few random choices of small pet names over the years. Esther had a Russian hamster called Frog and a toy tiger called

Duck. We had gerbils called Bubble and Squeak and various rabbits and guinea pigs with questionable names. A litter of three pups we had reared had been named Steak, Pie, and Chips, respectively.

We had a cat called Velcro, so named for its propensity to stick to the walls and soft furnishings. This cat had a habit of scooting up the chimney breast, which was covered in blown-vinyl wallpaper at the time. It would arrive at the top of the wall and anchor itself, crampon-style, with two clawed paws either side of the corner of the chimney breast. After glancing pointedly from side to side to see if anyone was going to be quick enough to retrieve it from the wall, it would then ski all the way back down, with its claws removing tramlines of textured wallpaper in its wake, creating a sort of polystyrene snow scene that showered anyone standing or sitting below. The party piece was best performed during Sunday lunch when everyone was jammed in around the table and no one could extract themselves quickly enough to save the wallpaper.

As a result of all these previous, dubious name choices, I was quite keen that we were not saddled with a completely ridiculous name for this new puppy, bearing in mind that there are occasions when one has to bellow in a public place to gain one's dog's attention and I didn't want to offend anyone.

The gorgeous, nine-week-old, black and white pup was placed on Naomi's knee, and she was completely mesmerised. At the time, she was twenty months old and had spent the recent Christmas season watching the Disney animation Mickey's Christmas Carol on repeat.

'What shall we call the puppy, Naomi?' we foolishly asked.

'Bah! Humbug!' she replied.

Philip brought home a kitten from a farm on one occasion and when this kitten and Humbug got a bit older they formed a team and hatched a plan that was mutually beneficial. Humbug spent a lot of time outside in her kennel and the cat, Tigger, was encouraged to lead a healthy, outdoor existence as well, mainly to preserve some sort of hygiene levels on my kitchen worktops. Sometimes, this arrangement wasn't to their liking and there were more and more occasions when we found that both animals were back inside the house without any of us having let them in.

The intriguing mystery was solved one day, after we were offered video evidence, taken by our neighbour, of the pets' activities. The back door handle had obviously had many years of use and abuse by that stage, with all our comings and goings, so the spring in the handle was less effective than it used to be. Tigger would jump up on to the outside handle and swing on it, pulling it down, although this in itself did not open the door. However, seeing the dilemma of the cat, Humbug would come along and helpfully push the door with her nose very firmly until it opened. Job done, the cat would drop to the floor and stalk inside after the dog, with her tail held high. This happened so frequently, once they had perfected the technique that I had to actually lock the door if I wanted them both to stay outside.

CHAPTER 23

Goodbye To Love

When my dad died

When Naomi was still very small, my parents announced that they were emigrating. Not that they were *thinking* of emigrating, but that it was all sorted, and they were going to live in South Africa in a couple of months' time.

They had both officially retired and would still receive their state pension even if they lived abroad, and they had been planning and making arrangements for the past year. The first I knew of it was when they came one day and told me that the passport and visa requirements had been met, they had made arrangements to initially stay with some people they knew over in South Africa, one way flights were booked, and they would be leaving in May.

It wasn't the best way to find out that sort of news, but it was no surprise. My mother had such a secretive streak, and she would have threatened my dad not to say anything to anybody, including me. He just wanted a quiet life, so he found it wiser to do as he was told. They had booked the removals company, who were tasked with packing up and emptying their house a couple of weeks before their flights were booked.

This left them homeless until the day they were due to go to the airport, so I was told they would stay with us. This arrangement proved to be an interesting one, as we had no spare rooms or beds and my mother was not one for blending in and 'going with the flow'. Philip and I ended up on an airbed in the playroom whilst my parents occupied our bedroom.

Not only that, I was the one, with four children in tow, who went to their empty house to clean it, ready for the people who had bought it. My mother did not consider it necessary to clean the house because it wasn't hers anymore, and she would be leaving the country anyway.

I admit to having many un-Christian thoughts and mutterings as I scraped many years of grease and dirt out of the kitchen cupboards. I was even more ungracious and nattered to myself quite a lot as I found myself vacuuming dog hairs off the stairs in their dormer bungalow.

I wouldn't have minded so much, but their dog had been dead for five years.

A couple of (fraught) weeks later, the airport minibus taxi arrived at our house at the appointed time, thankfully. The driver would have known about it, had he been late. There was much to-ing and fro-ing with luggage and coats and bits of this and bits of that, and finally, it was time for them to leave. My dad gave me a long, enveloping hug and got very emotional. He said goodbye to all the children and promised they would be back to see us. The last I saw of my mother before she went to live on the other side of the world, was of her standing on the pavement, instructing the poor taxi driver, in a loud, demanding voice, as to exactly where he should be putting her umbrella and camera case. She got into the minibus and just about remembered to wave out of the window as the taxi carried them off.

I was not even sure I would see my dad again, at that point. He had done remarkably well with his congenital heart condition until he reached the age of 50, when his incompetent aortic valve suddenly started to fail quite considerably. He was taken into Blackpool Victoria Hospital, which was the main adult cardiac centre for this area of the country, and he was given a valve replacement. It was a major operation and involved a lengthy, inpatient stay. It was a very worrying time, but he had pulled through, and he sported a large, impressive scar down the middle of his chest.

His rib cage had been closed with clips and, for a long time after, he used to set the alarms off when he went through customs checks at airports. These clips caused a few problems, though, and he had to go back to hospital a few years later for another operation to have them removed. He was permanently on Warfarin afterwards, to thin his blood to prevent clots forming on the valve. Whilst he lived in the UK, he had regular check-ups at the anticoagulant clinic at the hospital and his Warfarin dosage was constantly regulated to maintain his clotting levels. I don't know whether he had the same weekly checks in South Africa after they emigrated, but one Sunday lunch-time, whilst they were in a craft market, he collapsed and died instantly.

He had gone to church as usual that Sunday morning and had even conducted the choir, so it was a huge shock to everyone who knew him. We got a telephone call that afternoon on the 24th of November 1991 and it was in the days when you had one phone in the house which was always located in the hall and you sat on the stairs to take the call. I remember hearing Philip's side of the conversation as I sat at the top of the stairs whilst he spoke to my mother and shortly after I spoke to her myself, and she confirmed what had happened earlier that day.

Thankfully, I had seen my dad that same year. They had come over for a long holiday and stayed with us, so I had had the chance to spend some time with him. He had loved living in South Africa. He said he felt like he was permanently on holiday, but he clearly missed his family and his grandchildren.

We were in a quandary after that late afternoon phone call. We wanted to go over to South Africa for Dad's funeral, but we had no money for air tickets and, just as importantly, no valid passports. We had made enquiries and discovered that it was possible to go to Liverpool Passport Office, queue up, and get passports there and then, over the counter if you fulfilled their criteria.

Unbelievably, we were also offered the cost of our air tickets by our neighbour, who lent us his credit card and told us to pay him back when we were able. He wasn't just any neighbour. He and Philip had gone to school together, and he had been brought up on a farm at the other side of the village. He bought Lilian's house after she died, and got married soon after, so we have always had the privilege of having the best neighbours.

We set off for Liverpool at the crack of dawn on the Tuesday morning because it was going to take most of the day to get our passports renewed, and we had train tickets booked for later that evening, to get us down to Heathrow Airport to board a plane the following day. It was a long day, not without its complications, predictably, and a couple of hold ups but, by mid-afternoon, we were on our way back home, clutching our shiny, new passports.

We still could not just pack our cases and go, though. It was the end of a VAT quarter for the business and although, we had contacted HMRC and explained our predicament to the person who answered the phone, apparently, having my father die suddenly and having to make a hasty journey overseas, still did not excuse us from completing and submitting the all-important VAT return on time. They would brook no excuses so that evening saw us in the office upstairs at work, manually completing all the necessary forms so that our paltry contribution to the UK tax system would not arrive a minute late, owing to the fact we would still be out of the country in a few days' time, when it was due.

Philip's mum had already been installed at our house and was running the domestic activities, so we just had time to dash home, grab a bite to eat, throw some things into a suitcase and make the railway station in time to catch our midnight train. We arrived in London around 5:00 am and experienced the dubious pleasure of joining the subdued and surly commuters on the London Underground, to get across to Heathrow Airport. It was a dire journey, having been up all night already, with the prospect of the main journey still to come.

We caught our South African flight and landed in Johannesburg very early on Thursday morning. We had to take another, much shorter flight on to Cape Town and, by the time we arrived, we were nearly incoherent with exhaustion. The kindly folk at my parents' church had made arrangements for our accommodation, and we managed to get a few hours' sleep that afternoon. The funeral was the day after, on the Friday. It was strange because these folk had only known my dad for about two years, whereas all his lifetime friends were back home in England. Dad had obviously made an impression in his new church, though, and it was clear he was well liked and respected.

He was buried in a beautiful cemetery in Hout Bay, which was surrounded by elegant, fragrant eucalyptus trees and all the grave plot edgings were formed from pristine, white stones. His headstone was fashioned from dark grey marble and had a section of a musical score engraved into it, in recognition of what he loved to do best. Of course, it was gorgeous weather, it being their summer season. We had been transported in a matter of a few days, from dreary, dark, cold and rainy England in late November to a bright, sunny, hot South Africa which, under any other circumstances, would have been a wonderful experience.

We could not get our heads around the fact that when we went into the shopping areas over the next few days, all the shops were trimmed up with Christmas decorations because we were now into December, but the weather was sunny and hot, and we were going for walks on the beach.

A couple of days after we arrived back home in England, I received a letter from my dad. It had obviously taken two or three weeks to get through the South African postal system and it was most surreal to see his handwriting and read his account of the bonfire party and firework display they had attended earlier in November and of them driving back home along the coastal road in the moonlight with the lights twinkling over the bay. He wrote of having an excruciatingly sore throat and feeling quite ill with it. I have always assumed, because of that, that the infection he was suffering from had upset his blood coagulation levels and possibly a clot had formed that his artificial heart valve could not deal with, causing a massive and fatal heart attack. The South African authorities never came up with a definitive cause of death.

I missed my dad terribly, but I could never wish him back. He had been an absolute saint to live with my mother all those years, and I was so grateful that he did not have to live with constant conflict anymore and that now he had perfect peace. I do feel that my kids missed out, though. The older ones only have a handful of memories of a lovely, gentle man who taught them the basics of piano playing and gave them a £1 coin each before they went on holiday. This £1 coin would come with instructions 'to buy yourself an ice cream every day'. He was clearly out of touch with the inflationary cost of ice cream, even for those days! I don't know whether Naomi has any memory of standing next to his chair when she was only a toddler in the summer before he died, and cadging the toast he was eating for his breakfast. She was always rewarded by the last piece of every half slice being popped into her open mouth, with the topping he always referred to as Jarmalade. Naomi still called it that for a long time afterwards.

He was only 62 when he died, and he would have loved seeing his grandchildren grow up and would have been so proud of the people they married. He would have taken delight in his creative granddaughters-in-law and would have enjoyed spirited, theological debates with his grandsons-in-law.

CHAPTER 24

Sweet, Sweet Smile

*The face of a little girl who spent her
birthday in the Ronald McDonald House*

When Phil was twelve years of age, the team at Liverpool decided that the original patch they had repaired his coarctation with, had run the course of its efficacy, and they could no longer stretch any more room out of it. The time had come to perform further major surgery and replace the original patch with a bigger, more substantial one.

Of course, he was now far more aware of what went on during his hospital visits, so it was a daunting prospect for him, more so than his other admissions. The good news for us as parents, though, was that the whole of the paediatric cardiac unit had recently been moved to the Alder Hey Children's hospital on the other side of Liverpool and there was a new Ronald McDonald House on site which provided modern accommodation for patients' families.

The whole procedure was explained to us and, this time, to Phil himself. He was quite nonchalant about the prospect—after all, he had insider knowledge, thanks to his personal practical biology lesson, courtesy of the local abattoir. He wasn't unduly worried because the surgeons were the ones having to do the hard work, and he was only required to sleep through it all and for some time after. He could cope with that, he was well practised.

This repair would be achieved using calf pericardium. It was close to his own tissue in texture, and they were hoping to be able to fit a concertinaed, slightly larger than necessary, patch which would allow for a good amount of growing room. The surgical team were very optimistic that they would be able to perform an effective, semi-permanent repair that would see him through until he was an adult.

This was a much bigger operation than his previous one and took place during the first week of April in 1995. By this time, parents were allowed to play a much more significant role in their child's stay and treatment, consequently, Philip took Phil down to the operating theatre after his pre-med, whilst I stayed on the ward, quietly trying to maintain a strong, determined stiff upper lip, and failing miserably. We were able to spend the waiting time in much more pleasant and relaxed surroundings, this time, in the Ronald McDonald House.

There was a very large kitchen area, fitted out with six or eight bays of individual cooking and washing up areas. Each bay had its own fridge, oven with hob, washing up sink, worktop, and cupboards, each with adequate supplies of pots, pans and cutlery. There were corresponding tables where families could eat together if they wanted and further along the corridor, there were pleasant sitting areas with sofas and televisions.

These houses were so well thought-out and were, and still are, funded by charitable donations. It made a huge difference to the already traumatic time that parents spent at the hospital, not least because it was, at last, recognised that children in hospital were not just small adults, to be treated in an impersonal way and expected to get on with it. It had been realised by psychologists and clinicians alike, that children could suffer untold psychological issues as a result of being hospitalised for significant amounts of time in their formative years and their inpatient experiences had to be addressed and changed.

The attitude of the ward staff had changed considerably, and they chatted and conferred with the mums in a much more relaxed way. The senior ward sister even confided in me that the best way to maintain discipline in unruly patients was to use an orange in a sock. Apparently, it doesn't leave any bruises.

Good to know. She was joking, I hasten to add.

She had a very dry sense of humour and such a strong Liver-puddlian accent, it was difficult to catch everything she said. The sister was a very perceptive woman and also told me that almost all children who had experienced regular stays in hospital usually developed strong natural gifts to compensate. They were either arty or musical or could write poems and could use their talents as some sort of outlet whilst they were going through difficult and painful times.

Phil certainly had the musical gifting, which I am sure he inherited from both his grandads. Because I spent many days in hospital with him, I had borrowed a laptop, so I could do some work whilst I was in there. Our business did not run to such luxuries and laptops were a rare commodity in those days. Consequently, I was learning on the job and each time I made a mistake, the laptop would rat on me and tell the world using an electronic tone. Phil could tell me what exact note the laptop was sounding, and he also told me which two notes the ambulances produced as they arrived at, and left the hospital, using their emergency sirens. I checked when I got home, whether he really was pitch perfect, and he was. He has a tremendous musical talent and has played many instruments at one time or another, all self-taught.

Thankfully, this operation went without a hitch, but he was transferred to ICU for his post-op recovery. This time, it really was a distressing scene as we were admitted to the unit for the first time. He was connected up to every machine thinkable to keep track of, or support, all his bodily functions, and he was breathing via a ventilator. We could barely see him under all the equipment because he was so skinny. He had another scar now, just like his grandad's, right down the middle of his chest, where his heart had been accessed via his sternum.

When toddlers and babies are operated on, the ribs are soft enough for them to be prised apart and moved out of the way during cardiac procedures, hence his existing scar around his ribs from front to back. He had a bit of a pattern of scar lines going on now on his chest. I hadn't been able to stand and gaze at his chest for ages this time, pre-op, and lament the untouched landscape like I did when he was less than two years old. He was twelve now and wasn't about to tolerate his emotional mother gawping at his chest, no matter what the reason.

When he came round enough to have the ventilator removed the next day, he could see out of the window and started to look very confused. He asked me what date it was. I told him it was the 7th of April.

'No it's not,' he said.

'Yes, it is, why don't you believe me?' I asked.

'Look out of the window. It's snowing!' he said, clearly thinking he had been caught up in some sort of time warp and had woken up in winter. I looked out of the window and indeed, it was snowing in April. No wonder he was confused!

Philip was bringing Naomi with him when he came later in the day. The day after was going to be her birthday and as a treat we said she could come and sleep over that night, so she could wake up in the Ronald McDonald House on her birthday. The very serious reason why we were all in the hospital in the first place seemed to have escaped her—after all, it was only her brother who had been cut open, and the excitement of the visit overwhelmed her.

There were two single beds per family room (clearly Ronald McDonald was distancing himself from any responsibility of encouraging goings on which might possibly result in additions to the population), each with a truckle bed underneath that could be pulled out if siblings wanted to stay over, so Naomi had packed her things and arrived, ready to set up home in my room. We took her to see Phil with a little trepidation as we were not sure how she was going to react to seeing her brother looking so ill.

By now, Phil was sitting up in bed without his ventilator but still attached to numerous wires, tubes, and drains. He couldn't wear his pyjama top because of all the paraphernalia he was plugged into, so his large dressing was visible and some blood staining was obvious as it had seeped through. Naomi didn't bat an eyelid. She approached the bed cautiously, but was completely unfazed by all the unfamiliar equipment and started a conversation quite naturally with Phil, wanting to know what was under his dressing, and if she could have a look. She wanted to know what everything was for and what it was doing and where did it go to and, most importantly, did it hurt?

She soon lost interest in Phil and went off to find some more exciting things to keep her occupied, like toys. The good thing about taking children in to visit children was that there were always some toys to be found, even on the Intensive Care Unit. There was almost always a Play Specialist as well, who would admit any child to their play sessions, but as this was a Saturday, there was no one staffing the play equipment. Alder Hey took their children's education very seriously as they had a lot of long-stay patients and they had teachers who followed the school curriculum so that any loss of schooling could be kept to a minimum, if the child was well enough to participate in lessons.

When Naomi woke up the next morning, she was highly delighted to receive roller blades as her birthday present. The corridor outside the ICU was quite an undulating one and, it being Sunday, it was largely devoid of people and trolleys. It was an ideal opportunity for a little girl to learn to roller skate, and she set off with determination down the gently sloping corridor, slowly at first, then gathering speed and confidence as the morning wore on. I'm sure the Health and Safety Executive nowadays would frown on her activities and have her removed forthwith, but as it was, the doctors and nurses who narrowly avoided getting mown down by her somewhat erratic and unstable progress were very amiable and didn't seem to mind one bit.

After all, what was one more injured child to add to the number in the building? If you were going to do yourself a mischief, that hospital was the best choice of venue.

Phil's recovery was steady and good. The teachers sent work home for him, much to his delight, but when he did return to school, the members of staff were very reluctant to overtax him in any way. The PE department refused to let him do bleep tests, or any form of team game where he could not stop and rest whenever he needed to. They were scared stiff of him keeling over on their watch. Phil, of course, took full advantage of this situation, never having been one to use up one ounce of energy more than he really had to, and his joy at finally being able to avoid all forms of formal sport forever, was complete. He only had to sit down and sigh in a teacher's direction, and he would immediately be sent to the Medical Room for a lie down.

Neither did the orthodontist want any truck with him when our dentist referred him, regarding straightening his teeth during his teens. I filled in all the forms before the orthodontist examined him, and he did all the usual *humm*-ing and *haa*-ing as he worked his way around Phil's mouth. He was making all his recommendations about what he was going to do, until he read the medical history form which the nurse then showed him.

The orthodontist had an immediate U-turn in his deliberations, stopped totting up the hefty quote he had been planning to submit to the NHS in the interests of keeping his bank balance healthy and almost tipped Phil out of the chair.

'Ah, yes, well, actually, his teeth aren't all that bad,' he said, with a definite finality as he straightened himself up.

'I don't think it would be wise to risk disturbing any debris or infection that might be present in his mouth. We don't want any of that getting into his bloodstream and rushing straight to his heart, now, do we?'

For that, I translated: 'I'm not taking responsibility for him conking out whilst he's in my chair, thank you very much. I'll sign up another teenager who will be far less troublesome and I'll make my money in an easier way. Good day!'

As it turned out, Phil's teeth straightened themselves, so I was glad we hadn't contributed to any more stress in the orthodontist's life.

Phil's body's response to his major cardiac repair was extraordinary. He is now 37 and has never needed any more surgery, he has passed any medicals he has been sent for and his blood pressure does not cause him any trouble. He has never been ill, other than a seasonal cold or sore throat and has done his surgeons proud. God saw Phil through every procedure and has really looked after him in a miraculous way, for which we are very grateful.

CHAPTER 25

Yesterday Once More

*When we lost our business and were back
to square one*

Our lives were, like most people's, hectic, varied, stressful and sometimes just mundane. Generally, life was hard work and money was tight, with very few times of respite. It was almost impossible to relax or switch off from stresses because there was always a farmer ringing up for assistance or advice, even during important occasions. We cut short holidays and days out, and plans to go places or do things were invariably cancelled as soon as the next phone call came and weddings, celebrations, Christmas, Easter, and birthdays were hijacked, all in the pursuit of ensuring the cows got milked.

In the business, we had more than our fair share of customers who were quick to call Philip out but very slow and reluctant to pay him when the invoice dropped on their mat, but we also had a good proportion of honourable, dedicated farming families who acknowledged the worth of their dairy engineer and fully appreciated his commitment to them. Those were the ones who made a day's work worthwhile and kept him going, especially during mid-winter, out-of-hours callouts when the journey had already taken twice as long as it should have done and the road was barely visible through the rain-lashed windscreen or likely to disappear altogether into a snow drift. Over the years he was towed down many a farm track with a tractor, in order to get on or off the farm and endured many route diversions to avoid flooded roads or fallen trees, whilst the rest of the community who had finished their day's work were at home in the warm and dry.

The phone was known to ring at 11:00 pm and call him off to an emergency, only to ring again at 5:30 am, just a few short hours after getting back from the last farm, because another farmer's milking parlour wasn't doing what it was supposed to and there was a collecting yard full of bursting cows, desperate to be milked within the next couple of hours.

Whilst we had the usual domestic things going on in our personal lives, the agricultural world that supported our business was in crisis. The illness BSE (Bovine Spongiform Encephalopathy) had started to develop in cattle during the late 80s and by the mid-90s the impact on the farming community hit its peak. Farmers across the UK were instructed to slaughter their cows and all areas of the country were affected to a lesser or greater degree. Because a link had been suspected between a protein causing BSE infection and the human disease, CJD, the general public were reluctant to purchase and consume beef for fear of contamination and the EU had banned British exports worldwide. This ban continued for ten years, during which time, over one million animals were slaughtered and incinerated. Some countries even upheld the ban on British beef for many years after the official ban was lifted and continued to refuse to import our beef even though UK farming standards were, and still are, higher than most other countries'.

The effect this had on farming families was devastating. Many lost their businesses and consequently their homes, lots of farmers had to diversify to make ends meet and sadly, some farmers were so badly affected, they took their own lives. The smaller farms suffered the most and many did not survive the crisis and ceased to function as businesses. Subsequently, this hit our business very hard and we lost a lot of customers.

We still had all our business costs, wages, and overheads as well as a lot of debt outstanding from farmers who were never going to be in a position to pay us and, as a result, we lost our Porter's business in 1999.

Although it took many months to sort out all the details of wrapping up the business and making sure all the creditors had been paid—after the Tax man and the bank had been given priority, of course—the stark fact was, we still needed an income in the meantime.

Our farming customers that were still functioning continued to need engineering support for their milking equipment, so Philip's phone continued to ring.

Philip had been one of the first people to adopt the use of the new mobile phone system which, although slow to catch on and develop, had started to become very helpful to businesses in the UK since 1985. The original mobile phones had been hefty contraptions, made up of two parts: the receiver and the battery pack. They came in a case and it was like carrying a handbag around and they were incredibly cumbersome things. For an extra cost, you could purchase an aerial which clipped onto the outside of your work van, to give a better signal. Just how much better was debateable, especially in the highlands and lowlands of northern Lancashire and over into Yorkshire, where they had probably not got around to erecting any transmitter masts anyway, but it had its moments and had been handy on occasion.

Philip had been issuing his farming customers with his mobile number for quite some years, even though most farmers would no more ring a mobile phone number than move to live in the city.

By and large they did not trust new-fangled gismos, neither would they pay the extra cost of a mobile phone call over a landline call.

However, this innovative mobile phone came into its own and provided a system—albeit a reluctantly undertaken one—for the farmers to still be able to contact Philip and call him out to repair and service their equipment. It seems strange to think that these phones were revolutionary, not commonplace as they are today.

So, the following Monday morning after Porter's had closed, Philip went out to work for his existing customers as usual and he gradually set up another business in a self-employed capacity, based at home.

Even though we had lost our original business and livelihood, and were experiencing all the trauma that came with that complicated situation, we still knew God was in control. As Christians, we were not exempt from life's negative and sometimes disastrous circumstances, but we did have the reassurance that we were not going through it alone.

God does not send difficult times but He does allow them to happen, in order for us to grow in emotional and spiritual strength as we persevere through and learn from our experiences.

At that particular time in our lives, Philip was able to slowly develop another business with a slightly different approach but still using the skills and knowledge he had built up by trial and error and by taking whatever jobs came his way.

My life was also changing and, as the decade and century turned, I was about to find out what it was going to be like to be back earning a wage in the big, wide world, rather than working in the somewhat insular environment of the home and the family business.

On top of that, over the next few years, we, as a family, were to find ourselves in the middle of trials and tribulations that we never could have imagined.

Some people say that it would be good to know the future.

I would always dispute that and maintain that God knows best when He only allows us to experience one day at a time.

Certainly, if we had known what was about to happen in our lives, we would have found it almost impossible to deal with the prospect.

But that, as they say, is another story...

THE END